cave canem: V
2000 anthology

cave canem: V
{cc:v}

Cave Canem Workshop/Retreat
June 25 to July 2, 2000

ACKNOWLEDGEMENTS

"Not Forgotten" by Toi Derricotte was previously published in *Tender*, University of Pittsburgh Press.

"In A Place Where" by Patricia Johnson was previously published in *STAIN MY DAYS BLUE*, Ausdoh Press.

"In The Beginning" by Shara McCallum was previously published in *The Breadl Loaf Anthology of New American Poets*.

"Local Call" by Carolyn Beard Whitlow was previously published in *The Kenyon Review*, Volume XVIII, Number 1, Winter 1996.

Cave Canem: V / 2000 Anthology
ISBN 0-9709770-0-X

© Cave Canem 2001. All of the anthologized poets retain copyrights to their work.

CAVE CANEM 2000

FACULTY
Lucille Clifton
Toi Derricotte
Cornelius Eady
Michael S. Harper
Harryette Mullen
Tim Seibles

FELLOWS
Opal Palmer Adisa
Shane Book
Taiyon Coleman
Kamau Daa'ood
Omari C. Daniel
Eisa Davis
Jarita Davis
Pia Deas
Jarvis Q. DeBerry
Nelson Demery, III
T. Kebo Drew
Cherryl Floyd-Miller
Kendra Hamilton
Duriel E. Harris
Shayla Hawkins
Tonya C. Hegamin
Vida A. Henderson
Sean Hill
Yvonne Jackson
Jacqueline Johnson
Karma Johnson
Patricia A. Johnson
Douglas Kearney
Nzadi Keita
Janiece Kirton
Jacqueline Jones LaMon
Sherry Quan Lee
Reginald Lockett
devorah major
Dawn Lundy Martin
Phyllis McEwen
David Mills
Lenard D. Moore
Tracie Morris
Mendi Lewis Obadike
Gregory Pardlo
Carlo Paul
Nancy Shakir
giovanni singleton
Christina Springer
Lyrae Van Clief-Stefanon
Karen Wade
Marvin K. White
Carolyn Beard Whitlow
Angela A. Williams
Karen Williams
Treasure Williams
Bakar Wilson
Ronaldo V. Wilson
Yolanda Wisher
Toni Wynn

STAFF/BOARD
Desiree Cooper
michele elliot
Terrance Hayes
Carolyn Micklem
Sarah Micklem
Alecia Nails

table of contents

Opal Palmer Adisa	1	Unnerving 3
Jane E. Alberdeston-Coralin	3	For Julia de Burgos's "Rio Grande de Loiza"
Elizabeth Alexander	4	"The female seer will burn upon this pyre."
Holly Bass	5	better roses
Herman Beavers	6	Vernell Contemplates the Meaning of Existence
Shane Book	8	Offering
Toni Brown	10	
Stephania Byrd	11	Bitter Savory
Robin M. Caudell	12	Delilah's End-Time Song
Taiyon Coleman	14	standard one
Desiree Cooper	15	Ode to an English garden
Teri Ellen Cross	16	Complected
Omari Daniel	17	God Fool All Six Foot Three Two Hundred Eighty Black Pounds of Me
Eisa Davis	18	Muzz Crick
Hayes Davis	19	September
Jarita Davis	20	Nasturtiums at Giverney
Pia Deas	22	That Way
Jarvis Q. DeBerry	23	sanctified
Nelson Demery III	24	The Eyes of My Beholders
Toi Derricotte	26	Not Forgotten
Ronald Dorris	27	St. Philip Blues

T. Kebo Drew	29	Reiki: a laying on of hands
Cornelius Eady	31	Photo of the Young Freddie Hubbard
michele elliot	32	landscape 4
Phebus Etienne	34	Najee's Visit
Cherryl Floyd-Miller	35	monkey love
Kendra Hamilton	36	What's Inside
Michael S. Harper	37	Sherley Anne Williams: 1944–1999
Duriel E. Harris	39	"Academy of War": A March ad majorem Dei gloriam (Rondeau) (after unseen photograph by Linda Bertucci)
Reginald Harris	40	Sunday Brunch
Shayla Hawkins	43	Wet Places
Terrance Hayes	44	The Things-No-One-Knows Blues
Tonya C. Hegamin	46	
Vida Henderson	47	The Tree on Guillot Road
Sean Hill	48	Uncle John
Major Jackson	49	viii. Block Party
Yvonne A. Jackson	50	Underwear
Valerie Jean	51	Another Version
Brandon D. Johnson	52	Past Time
Jacqueline Johnson	54	Bruised Fruit
Karma Johnson	56	
Patricia Johnson	59	In a Place Where

A. Van Jordan	61	The Journey of Henry "Box" Brown
Douglas Kearney	62	Anansi Meets Peter Parker at the Taco Bell on Lexington
Nzadi Keita	64	what does it take
Janiece Kirton	66	
Jacqueline Jones LaMon	67	white butterfly
Sherry Quan Lee	68	Bruise Number Two
Reginald Lockett	72	The Dumb Class
Doc Long	74	Rules for Cool
devorah major	75	crops not harvested
Dawn Lundy Martin	77	(F)
Shara McCallum	79	In the Beginning
David S. Mills	80	Hide and Seek
Veronica Mitchell	84	Mea Culpa
Lenard Duane Moore	85	On First Reading the Introduction to Natural Birth by Toi Derricotte
Renée K. Moore	88	Eurydice
Tracie Morris	89	Combinations
Harryette Mullen	90	The Fire This Time
Mendi Lewis Obadike	91	Tell me this is because we remember long
Gregory Pardlo	92	Pyro
Carlo Paul	94	The poem on your door
Hermine Pinson	95	Redemption Song

Cherise A. Pollard	101	Call and Response
Ro-Lyan Reid	102	This Hour, When I Am Minute
Millicent Rucker	104	New Year's Eve
Tim Seibles	105	The Further Adventures of Tutor the Turtle
Nancy Mebane Shakir	107	Ancestors
Evie Shockley	109	apprenticeship
giovanni singleton	111	emerald
Mistinguette Smith	112	Brunette
Christina Springer	114	Behind His Back, I Call Him Sambo
Imani Tolliver	116	smoke
Lyrae Van Clief-Stefanon	122	For My Husband's First Love
Karen Wade	124	When the Wind Blew the Door Open
Jay Ward	125	An Untitled Fugue
Afaa M. Weaver	127	Composition for White Critics…
Marvin K. White	133	Jitter
Carolyn Beard Whitlow	135	Local Call
angela williams	136	What Words
Karen Williams	139	Offerings
Lorelei Williams	141	Domestic
Shannon Williams	142	Leaves
Treasure Williams	143	Bull Dagger
Bakar Wilson	145	Dream Cognition

Ronaldo Wilson	147	Two Sequences from *The Urticaria Series*
Bridgette Wimberly	149	REVERSE DISCRIMINATION ain't no such thing
Yolanda Wisher	153	Ruby Flo
Vincent Woodard	158	bloodbrother ritual 2
toni wynn	160	i value safety
Group E Collective Poem	161	We Are Thankful For Lucille Clifton
Cave Canem	163	Cave Canem Renga

Opal Palmer Adisa

Unnerving 3

she understood
that she did not understand
what they were talking about
no more than they understood
what they thought she had said
when she hadn't spoken
understanding
was not the problem

why tell the truth
if a lie adds more clarity
her heart was beating
yet she had not outlived her time

she chewed the insides
of her cheeks
chewed
and chewed
until all the saliva was gone

they had to make it complex
pretending to fix
what they could never repair
fearing
the fear
of what they didn't know
beyond imagining

someone has to be always
chasing someone

or their shadow
she didn't cut her eyes
or suck her teeth
she gasped

she was trying
really hard
to not lose it
not lose it
don't lose it
the very idea was ludicrous
but she tried anyway
until it erupted
in her mouth
and her laughter detonated

Jane E. Alberdeston-Coralin

For Julia de Burgos's "Rio Grande de Loiza"

Dismay turned your waters black to blood
but of the many who sought your bottomlessness
one lowing you remember
her voice petalled like the fur of the flamboyan
calling through an aboriginal dream

Angels sift your waters with pelican wings

Through the Yunque's wildness
your depths are dredged in search of her
the tide arouses the bones of the disappeared
lovelorn opaled, wet and rising
skins a vellum on your tangled floor

how long since anything sweet
has fallen into that muscular lapping?
A month's turn finds your love
her limp betrayal dressed in algae

your heart bursts
you go blind
hunger perverts you
you lose your step
Witches toss orange blossoms into you
    call you Moncho, Dario, German

nothing but death names you
your poet is gone
and all the bodies that surface are Caribe

Elizabeth Alexander

"The female seer will burn upon this pyre."

Sylvia Plath is setting my hair
on rollers made from orange juice cans.
The hairdo is shaped like a pyre.

My locks are improbably long.
A pyramid of lemons somehow
balances on the rickety table

where we sit, in the rented kitchen
which smells of singed naps and bergamot.
Sylvia Plath is surprisingly adept

at rolling my unruly hair.
She knows to pull it tight.
                                            Few words.
Her flat, American belly,

her breasts in a twin sweater set,
stack of typed poems on her desk,
envelopes stamped to go by the door,

a freshly-baked poppyseed cake,
kitchen safety matches, Black-eyed Susans
in a cobalt jelly jar. She speaks a word,

"immolate," then a single sentence
of prophesy. The hairdo done,
the nursery tidy, the floor swept clean

of burnt hair and bumblebee husks.

Holly Bass

better roses
Georgia, August 1999

Driving home from the city, I tell my father I'd like a piece of cotton to take back. We stop along the road. He tells me how during harvest he picked cotton every day after school. Five-and-a-half cents per pound. The most in one day? 217. Forty years later, he still remembers this number. Still remembers the excitement of seven hard-earned dollars in his hand.

I open my car door. I'll get it, Daddy says. Whatchu want? Just a cotton boll? He looks across the field for signs of shotgun-toting, overzealous farmer. No one in sight. He wades through high grass in dress slacks and good shoes. I pray the ground is dry.

He pulls off three nice bolls. From where I am, it looks like he is picking small, white roses for me. He returns to the car and places them in my hands. I examine these strange flowers, turning them by the stem. The papery leaves crumble at my touch, revealing the hard hull. Pointed enough to draw blood, dark as my own skin.

Herman Beavers

Vernell Contemplates the Meaning of Existence

We was lookin at the Discovery Channel.
some program with this philosopher
cat talkin bout fallin into the Abyss.

He called that shit,
A place where Man wallows in despair...
Man's pain multiplied unto infinity...
A place you reach only after
stumbling through life's obstacles
without a spiritual map.

Jean thumped the back of Vernell head, say
Every woman live wid a nigga
don't put the seat down at night
know what the man talkin bout.

Well, Vernell, he listen for a while
then he turn to me and Jean, and say,
Damn, I wonder how far you got
to drive before you run up on the Abyss?

Now, if he had thought about it,
he mighta said somethin like:
Our journey into the [abyss] is not
a journey in space, but a journey in spirit.

Or he coulda put on
his Heidegger Jones and said:

**So the meaning of Being
Must already be available to us
In some way. As we have intimated,
We always conduct our activities
In an understanding of Being
And the tendency that leads us
Towards its conception.**

but he didn't say none a that shit.
Instead, he say,

*Hey I wonder can you get there off 271?
Is it a big hole what don't have no bottom?
Is getting there like ridin the Jackrabbit at Euclid Beach?
Is it anywhere near Canton?*

*Last time I was out that way,
they was workin on the highway.
I hit a detour and drove in
circles around that shit for days.
Ended up somewhere out by West Hell.
I bet I was right at the Abyss
and din't realize that shit!*

Naw, Vernell, I say,
you was in Akron.

*Yeah, you must be right, Drew,
Anything look like the Abyss
got to be out past Toledo.*

*Damn let me call my cousin in
Destroy. I bet that nigga
know how to get there.*

Shane Book

Offering

At the beach, I once saw my father, surrounded by a crowd,
put his lips over the mouth of a man lying prone on the sand.

There was something in the way he worked, quickly but precisely,
and without flourish. He could have been nailing shingles,

or measuring slabs of gyprock for our grey clapboard house
that leaned into the North Vancouver drizzle long before

we got there. As a child, it always seemed to be raining,
so that now, years later, returning to the city, it is somehow

strange to be sitting on a woman's bed in a small apartment
in a warm square of late afternoon sun. And perhaps

because of the warmth on my skin, I do not think of when
we lived in that rundown house on that street where the neighbours

wrote Nigger Go Home in jaunty chalk letters that stretched
to our lane. I do not think of my mother speaking in the kitchen

late at night of our leaving, my father forever silent,
in what I came to imagine was the thin music of shame.

Why should I? At this moment, a woman is getting ready
to step out of the bathroom wearing nothing but a silk Japanese

smoking jacket, and when she does, she will stand blinking
in the bright light, then let her robe fall away,

and in that instant her white skin will shine in the afternoon light.
At this moment, I have not yet placed my hands on her neck,

cradling it, the way my father held the man at the beach, long after
he realized his breath in those dead lungs was helping nothing

and finally, he quit. The man on the beach would never return
to the earth he was born of. And I too have quit, by leaving.

Which is why I cannot tell you, father, of my own encounter
with shame. How brown my hands look on her,

and in their stillness, how useless. This bright offering
I am unable to take, this pale one that lights up the room.

Toni Brown

Return
Pushed from the belly of a silver bird
I follow the others into the light
Yours is the first face I see.
Claim me with a kiss
that is long and indulgent, unmindful and dangerous
then turn, I will follow you anywhere.
You carry one bag
I bring the other to the car, where your voice
touches me like hands.
Leave the windows open wide
Let the roar of the city and the sidewalk's smells
wash over my skin, enter.
Climb the stairs, unlock the door
Leave the suitcases just inside our first room
Hardwood squeaks mark our steps.
Take off my clothes like a child
Pull them over my head or down to the floor
Let your fingers read me.
I still smell of sage
see pine covered mountains when I close my eyes
My lips feel dry against your mouth.
Lick me back into this world
Call my outlaw name in our native tongue
Help me remember who I am.

Stephania Byrd

Bitter Savory

A growing woman sweeps up her tooth and nails
in a Dutch-oven of dreams
where courting sparks shy laughs, ringing in the bottle trees.
If things aren't going to work out,
and no one knows what's hurting or going begging,
she can eat misunderstanding, dry on crackers,
but with a taste for something fresh-picked.
Witness in a bottle of everlasting spirit
does not have the same flavor. Even with pain,
there is nothing quite like the first yield
for remembrance
and the late-bearing
to fill out a stew.

Robin M. Caudell

Delilah's End-Time Song

I didn't know
if you were kissing
your brother,
friend, or lover
or all three,
Manoah's son.
Like picking pennies tails-up,
it doesn't matter anymore.
I still cannot say your name
or open a sand dollar
without breaking it
(like I did you)
or dip its petals
in five oceans
take what rattles inside
place it in the hand
of a ragged man, say,
this is hope for
the next 1,000 years.
I didn't know you
but I smelled your hair
that made you strong
that made me wrong you
in Sorek Valley.
No shears,
I cut your hair
with my tongue.
Your clippings curl
in a blue glass jar with sage.
I burn it still.

Call it love.
You told me
my hands were light
easy to hold like chamomile
in a wooden sieve over a porcelain cup.
I drank that like lamb's blood.
It was never enough.
I saw you there in St. Mark's Place
beneath the last full moon
of this 1,000 years
and I wanted to ask you
if you remembered
gouged eyes, bronze chains,
Gaza or grinding grain
but you were saying
good-bye
to your brother,
friend or lover
so I passed you
holding the hand
of another
seven-locked man.

Taiyon Coleman

standard one

now falling low
the sky shade splits
between light blue
pink lavender
and the promised white
of the next day's sun

below
miembe[1] and migomba[2]
fires are burning
two boys hurry   majirani[3]
and I watch them
trail through trash
weaving tall grass
and houses held together

walking
one is a primary
school boy
his uniform still on
carrying a smaller fire
in twisted newspaper

in his other hand
he is bringing
a grease container
full of liquid
for the night's washing
ugali meals
and his family's thirst

---

[1] mango trees
[2] banana trees
[3] neighbors

Desiree Cooper

Ode to an English garden

we were tempted to take off our shoes
let our toes remember
the rich black-coffee heat
of the midday soil
drink in the daisies
floating yellow as lemon rinds
in a jelly jar of tea
hike our skirts high
and run through the pink delphinium
gather up the coneflowers and lay their healing
on each others' lips
let leaves of sage
dry pungent in our pockets
rescue the tight, nappy head of purple cabbage
and take it back home
to the snap beans and turnips
where it belonged.

But a sign reminded, "Please do not touch the plants."
we left, our lungs full of roses and lavender,
knowing there wasn't a plant in their garden
our mothers' hands
hadn't already touched.

Teri Ellen Cross

Complected

What the fine rain does not hide and cannot wash away
are coal fingers shrugging slicker strings tighter,
protecting just-straightened hair. The humidity

is deadly to this delicate process,
and can nap the nape along the kitchen instantly,
reverting to the natural curl she dreads.

The girl beside her wears no slicker but has a ponytail
like Barbie's and is just as fair. The pubescent boys stare.
She's an urban Venus, impossibly waiting for the same bus.

The hooded girl is not Venus. Dark brown is not beauty—
darker still a death sentence if you are young, waiting
for a bus, a long appreciative glance, even catcalls, "hey redbone"—love.

The hooded girl hopes the Korean store up the street
will have a sale soon on fading cream and human hair,
because, beauty here is serious business.

Omari Daniel

God Fool All Six Foot Three
Two Hundred Eighty Black Pounds of Me

God quit playin spades
Put down the Boones Farm and rot gut
Remove this hangover
Start removing vomit from eyes
So when people see me they see
Intelligence first, then a teacher, a poet
Let them touch me out of anything other than curiosity
Assume I am fragile and vulnerable too
Don't transform me into a forklift, a ladder, a pillow

Give me a chance to be small

Approach me in darkness and see me
Take away my danger sign
Take away my caution flag
Don't yield

God show me this killer they see
Not the man who last fought in grade school
Because some one called his mother Nigger
Show me the ball player they see
Not the man whose momma kept him off the field
Oh, and please God show me the giant dick they see
Not the man generous enough to compensate with his tongue
Show me the spear-chucking rapist they see
Anything but all six foot three
two hundred eighty black pounds of me.

Eisa Davis

Muzz Crick
from *Bulrusher*

I float in a basket toward the Pacific, hands
blue as huckleberries. This air is too sweet,
this cold water a thin, foul milk.

The woman who bore me wrapped me,
gave me to the green of the Navarro,
named me silence. She prays

this river has studied time
and will never turn back
her secret skin, the mark

that stretched into life.
Forgiveness is an insect
that may one day draw my blood.

Catch me, I ask the black power lines,
defying the fog's quiet shroud. What is
a motherless daughter but pure will?

The river turns to molasses.
With a sharp bank through high shams,
I am born into a new language.

This is from a series set in Northern California's wine country, where residents in a small town developed a unique dialect at the turn of the last century called Boontling. Some of its terms appear in the poems.

bulrusher: a foundling, an illegitimate child.
muzz crick: a swollen or flooded waterway.
Navarro: a river adjacent to Boonville.
shams: brush, weeds.

Hayes Davis

September

In the middle of a sentence of advice, the first wave
takes his legs as if the salt water were in league
with the diabetes. For the first time you see your father

fall. Sitting on the wet sand, his legs covered with the surf,
he laughs. It's genuine, not the uneasy, self-deprecating
chuckle he used to relate the story of the day last summer

when he wet his pants. The next wave comes as he's
struggling to stand up, gripping the hand you've extended
and as this wave takes him from your grasp you feel a little

of what it might be like when he slips more finally away.
The wave rolls him towards the beach and he comes to rest
again, this time on all fours and not laughing. His hair

is damp, white with sand. He sputters water from his mouth.
And before he tries to stand again the wave recedes,
taking him with it. So, like a catcher blocking home

you stand in front of him, stopping him with words you
thought were made only to be spoken back: "I've got you."
Then the sea relaxes, lets you help him up. Part of you feels

proud, like you've passed a test. Part of you wants to fall,
let him pick you up once more. Later, you watch him sleeping
with his back to you, stretched on the blanket, his description

of feeling "helpless" still echoing uncomfortably. But you
remember that he lent you $40 this morning, looks good for his
age, and could still take care of you, if you needed him to.

Jarita Davis

Nasturtiums at Giverney

Poker chips scatter along the edge of my porch
green disks sway, nasturtium leaves cross into darker
shades, or separate, sun shining beneath larger
leaves, tarnished half dollars, spread the pigment thinner.

I was fifteen when Mrs. K, neighbor, Jr. High
drama coach, knew I needed the theater. Yale
Rep's opening night. Midsummer's Night Dream. Hidden
lamps behind green umbrellas: pea, moss, bottle, pale.

Nasturtiums stand in watercress salads, flowers
for food at restaurants which my mother, almost
disgusted, and certainly unimpressed declared
those things "for rich people." But here, these leaves, posted

in pulsing colors, Monet's bridge over wet blue
and green on the notecards I bought at the MoMA.
The toreadors' red capes across black velvet
canvas hung in our family room did not lead

me to consider the play of horizontal
waters and bridge with the trees' vertical drooping
or grasses leaning tall and lazy beneath leaves
puffing up in curls, foaming edges in silver.

I thought, "I want to write like that," my eyes blurring
the image or the images blurring my eyes
Mrs. K beside me, my face wet, my head thick
from crying. Puck's forest, pine and leaves in darkness.

But it wasn't that painting, the one with the bridge,
That was only a card I sent once, hoping all
was well. The words were kind, if transparent, hoping
his family was happy, healthy. No return

address, I was beguiling, thinking he'd miss me
if he couldn't contact me. Thinking we could share
that, at least but mostly I spared myself waiting
to understand that he would never respond.

Trembling green wafers eclipse each other. Above
the nasturtium leaves' taut pulses, a heavy, pale
head holds itself upon a long neck. Lips, clenched around
the pursed, wrinkling orange, waiting to push forward.

The MoMA held walls of water lilies, I leaned
closer. How to create a hushed image without
painting it, exactly? A figure in the top
right corner, fishing. Blended in dollops: leaves, sky.

The guards watched. I clasped my hands behind my back, one
holding the wrist of another. My mother sighed
"that's for rich people," from somewhere. The guards didn't
hear. Nose inches from the canvas, I peered closely

between black and green and blue splotches and found orange.
That's how you have to do it, I thought. Dab orange
where you only expect green. Stepping back, the wet
trees' reflections hovered over it, lost in the lake.

I can't expect for the nasturtiums I planted
in late August to survive the cold. I won't wait
to be disappointed by the cautious flowers.
Only chlorophyll, dense and clotted in leaf tips.

Pia Deas

That Way

You say I'm not as tender as I used to be.
Perhaps.
I know that often I'm tense, closed off.
I notice it even in my voice, like this morning
When I spoke the word "way," not from my body, but
From the space between my throat and head.

It's hard to go deeper.
I can't force the "way" down to my belly
but, if for example, I say, "water, water, water"
I begin to reconnect. And when you say
"Baby"
In that way you do,
My secret reservoir breaks.

Jarvis Q. DeBerry

sanctified
>for marvin

Count it not idolatry.

Though I kneel
And drink from a cup
of viscous liquid love,
entangle myself
within the brown limbs
of supple, willing flesh,
I am praising You, Dear Father,
yielding worshipfully to
the bewildering beauty
of Your sweet feminine creations.

When my tongue finds sanctuary
In nubile bosoms
and I lap up the salty sweat of passion,
turn away thy wrathful gaze
and know, O Merciful One,
that I have no other gods before Thee.

But in my lust for spiritual truth
I lean toward this understanding,
That not even
the blood
of the Lamb
washes out these Solomonic desires
so I seek Your Holy Spirit
in Your temples of flesh and bone.

Nelson Demery III

The Eyes of My Beholders

I tired of the mirror
my reflection's pouting lips
that cover chipped and crooked teeth;
zits, dents, blemishes, and hairbumps pimpled like hills and valleys
sunken eyes
too small for seeing
under a long and swollen forehead (…it's the black kid from Mars
nigger Martian not green, nigger Martian not green…)
and the nose Mother never could pinch
into perfection

so, I became
a vampire
and now that the mirror casts no memory of my ugly image
I awaken by the glint of moonlight
penetrating the slits
of my bedroom venetian blinds
dress in clothing too small
to cover me, tight enough
to reveal the figure
of a thinly slimmed agile creature
who roams and creeps unstarred nights
guided by a beacon of streetlights
in search of victims to drain.

A vampire
I suck
out their life-force
relinquish them of their strength
while, spellbound and stumbling

they caress my hair and tell me
I am magic
I am sexy
I am very good
I am just right
I am too much
I am perfect
I am oh God, oh yes that's it!

Then, with the blank death-stare in their eyes as my proof
I return home in need of no reflection, believing
I am   severely
beautiful.

Toi Derricotte

Not Forgotten

I love the way the black ants use their dead.
They carry them off like warriors on their steel
backs. They spend hours struggling, lifting,
dragging, so that even the dead will be of service.
It is not grisly—as it would be for us—
to carry them back to be eaten. I think of
my husband at his father's grave—
the grass had closed
over the headstone and the name had disappeared. He took out
a pocket knife and cut the grass away; he swept it
with his handkerchief to make it clear. "Is this the way
we'll be forgotten?" And he bent down over the grave and wept.

Ronald Dorris

St. Philip Blues

It was Sunday
she had on Billi's dress
and wore Lena's look
some little girl grown up to be
big sportin' her stuff
in a garden in New Orleans
around the corner from Bayou St. John
with melody floatin' in the air
and Magnolia smellin' up the place

who would have thought
one and a half years ago
when she came ridin' in
on a note of Delta distinction
that she would go out so grand
a star at a filmmaker's house
singin' that old familiar tune
if it ain't broke, baby
then don't fix it
as the black dog barks
and the neighborhood children
on a wing and a prayer
shout as she opens the gate
to let in the artist from St. James
who painted the *tignon* queen

often my grandmother
told me stories like this
about women who came
floatin' down the Miss'sippi
with a gardenia in their hair
whistlin' they got rhythm
who could ask for anything mo'

oh, but *mais oui, chère*
the night was young
the June bugs were jumpin'
and Philli-man had the flash rollin'
technology in the dark, he said
that could capture any moment
so as not to miss
the rose petal attraction
in baby doll pink
on a sea of sky blue satin

don't get nuttin' on that dress
the crowd yelled
lift up that skirt, baby
so it won't trail the dust
turn to the downriver side
give us that best pose
show us what yo' mamma gave you
'cause it's Sunday, darlin'
and you got on that Billi dress
and wearin' that Lena look
some little girl grown up to be
big sportin' her stuff.

T. Kebo Drew

Reiki: a laying on of hands

My hands be shining
from the pulsar core
of my palms

my hands
so elegant like
my grandmother's

my hands
on Black women's bodies
reaching through their skin
to that flower petal place
next to the vital organs

my hands be shining
my hands be feeling

that this sistah needs to breathe
with a tree
exchange breath with the shaggy
leaf green head whisperer
like she's got a right
like that's her job
and breathing
is her way to make a living

my hands be feeling
that this sistah need
soft tenderness
like the place
at dawn
where the blues and gospel meet

my hands be shining
like they sho nuff working with God

Cornelius Eady

Photo of the Young Freddie Hubbard

On the appropriate shoulders,
Even the blues can be a pretty thing.
If strut,
Spent women and cigarettes
Have a sound,

Then somebody, (please),
Hand this man a trumpet,
Young funk poured into a sharp pin-stripe.

He smiles at the hungry club.
See what you have done.
He's about to raise his horn.
O, see what you have done.

michele elliot

landscape 4

Yvonne and her husband pick me up from the airport in casper wyoming
on the ground the white of the clouds is still blinding.
cows like dice in a hand are strewn haphazardly across
the flat parts of this land, the sky stretches forever
rolling plains like waves of green and brown alongside the road
it's hard for me to distinguish the animals grazing against the
roadside, my eyes are not yet sharp enough to pick them out
rock formations, Yvonne calls them stone cities
I can pick out the Russian olive trees
the hills like brown bodies lay entwined naked
the curves and crevices, folds of flesh lying together
legs and shoulders, butts and backs and thighs, brown breasts and stomachs
we're headed toward the mountains pink and purple and white, grey edges
in the distance and the sun is setting

black angus black velvet dots closely nestled against dry brittle brown grass
middle fork road, south fork, crazy woman canyon
the mountains are a dark shadow, black like me
it's better to be black out here than native American

Phebus Etienne

Najee's Visit

The youngest relative, drool bubbling
down his chin, jiggled as his dimples
met my mother's lips. "Najee," she smiled,
her hand squeezing his hamhock thigh.

Last August, as she changed his diaper,
she encouraged him to shit on me for luck,
so that I could bring to her a replica of me.
She joked then, that I had no husband

because I wore my skirts too long,
that she would die before I married,
then promised me a champagne bath
with chants on New Year's Eve,

a Haitian remedy certain to end my solitude.
The baby grabbed the sunset tulips painted
on the comforter. My mother's shaky soprano rose
with the same refrain she sang to me

in Mahotier when I was new,
when she scrubbed me clean
in the tin basin filled from the stream,
the water dappled with lemon leaves.

Checking the folds behind Najee's ear,
she proclaimed that he would
remain the color of pecans. Already
I was missing the things she could teach.

Fading sunlight ringed my last gift,
an amaryllis named for the moon.

Cherryl Floyd-Miller

monkey love
(from *the adulteress series*)

red want. ruby. prize forbidden fop.
coils at inflections. coy.
kingdom class order
family species: married man.
coupling vernacular. apple-shiny eyes.
cagey gold band. booty. indigenous tongue.

Kendra Hamilton

What's Inside

i

I am little and I dream my grandma dead.
I hold a hairpin to my teeth, bite the plastic
from the tips.
In my hand it is a sword.
By my hand grandma will die—
Right after my bath in the big tin tub.

ii

Daddy's sister is a fat yellow cow.
When Mama says so, Daddy gets mad.
Daddy's sister says I am spoiled.
Makes me stay inside.
Lets her kids play outside.
Daddy's sister talks, talks, talks all day,
says bad things about my ma.
Daddy's sister is a fat yellow cow.
I say it, and Daddy slaps my face.

iii

I love my daddy. Daddy loves grandma.
If I kill grandma, must I kill him, too?

iv

In our kitchen drawer, there's a sharp, sharp knife.
It cuts through butter like it's hot.
I am little and I dream I'm slicing down.
It cuts through like it's hot.
I open the drawer sometime, to be sure it's there.
The edge is sharp.
I put it back.

Michael S. Harper

Sherley Anne Williams: 1944–1999

Worshiped
in the fields

sometimes
in darkness

heat
at highnoon

killing fields
but after water

fluorescent
crops

braceros
picked

you sent me a tape
short and full

of healing music
(I copied it for my mother)

put you in every book
I could read or write

remember
your commentaries

at public
tables

in and out
of the university

outtakes are best
your heart a map

ancestors weeping

Duriel E. Harris

"Academy of War": A March ad majorem Dei gloriam
(Rondeau)(after unseen photograph by Linda Bertucci)

allegro

strike	piece	hang	glee
rally	bright	block	fend
grit	sap	moil	ditty
raze	swell	drench	wax

strike	piece	hang	glee
pack	gut	steer	paste
mar	mold	thud	vault
bare	muck	ardor	blood

strike	piece	hang	glee
grease	scourge	gleam	knot
pus	sole	drought	lean
thumb	sack	skull	pitch

strike	piece	hang	glee
pierce	scrap	pool	skein
wreck	dredge	strut	sear
shaft	hinge	grid	rack

strike	piece	hang	glee

Reginald Harris
Sunday Brunch

Eastern Shore continued:
    The **sun** is shining   this after
        Noon every shadow's dangerous   in
                Howard Johnson's lobby

calling out your name   to fellow travelers
    A Seminar on Time and how   to slice   it   lemon
      wedges or two   three-minute eggs   where my parents met

Tell: Where are you headed? Show me off to town
    Is there butter on the table any comics
        on the page   Any making their own days around the edges,

under the arcades   such desolation makes
    a better life   one becomes more conscious
                of the words   of the ways   of what one knows
                                             and says   says what one

would have been so long ago   should
      have said   for I am so in love and   give the liar's kiss
            out of it   all melted into air   *My name is on the wheat*
                                that says I love you

bread Ration List (one day only for us   the enslaved)
    Shine like the moon sufficient
        for all the work that's done   and yet too much   the riches
                            of the Earth, begging, destitute   a child

Looks like you're writing a letter—Would you like help?
    restore to you the years the locusts ate   orange juice
            and champagne   homemade jam   the detritus
                                of mornings outside Cambridge   *Go Down*
                                                                 Moses

Say a prayer Dregs in the cup Rocks Ashes and the lure Why, oh tell me
　　　　　　　in my bed　　　　　　　　　　of meaning Why don't we
　　　　　　　　　　　　　　　　　　　　　　　　　　　　　go out?

Shayla Hawkins

Wet Places
Salto La Coca, El Yunque, Puerto Rico

The waterfall is a long silver tongue
running over the mountain,
smoothing her rough body,
crying the tears her stone face
cannot release.

The waterfall is washing the mountain,
draping her nakedness,
sending the dirt that covers her
back to the earth,
banishing her fear
like leaves on the wind,
like forgiven sin.

The waterfall's moist kiss
is teaching the mountain to trust,
to know that when she comes
to the wet places,
she will survive
and her body will soften into song.

Terrance Hayes

The Things-No-One-Knows Blues
after Wanda Coleman

I filed for bankruptcy in the borough of luxury.
I suspect it's time to eat my poetry.
My favorite turtleneck sweater, the green,
50% rayon, 5% cotton (rest unknown) one,

shrank in a tub of hot
bath water. A prisoner bit
a chunk out of my step-daddy's smile.
My mamma filled

her cancer with silicon &
pity. My wife dwells in
a house of critics. I'm younger than
sugar, but older than

NutraSweet cause I just had a birthday in
New Orleans.
I suffer various degrees
of wistfulness.

Honey,
I guess it's time I eat my poetry.
Cranked to ten my *Walkman* screams
static. I believe B.B. fingered

Lucille like the back of a pretty woman's knee,
but no one seems to agree.
Need pecks at the latch
of my *Wal-Mart* wristwatch.

The lines on my palms slope like portable ex
& why graphs. Baby, I suffer various degrees
of wistfulness. I suspect my penis will
be fed to a swimming Gila

monster. Death
calls me occasionally collect.

Tonya C. Hegamin

from Black Feathers on Concrete

I.

She goes to bed each night placing debris, articles of clothing and shoes strategically so that when the rapist comes he might alert her to his eminent arrival. She tells visitors of her dubious plan so that they do not think her untidy. She tells them with a serious face that piling runs in her family so that they might nod out of sympathy at the mountains of junk. But none of this will ever truly fool the rapist killer. He laughs outside of her ground level windows at her earnest attempts. Of course he has mapped out where each telltale sock and empty box lies in wait for his false step.

II.

Of course he has no false steps. He has different pairs of shoes to walk around in as not to be clearly identified. She wonders which footprint in the backyard he belongs to. He is crafty. When she looks he is not there. She is crafty. She tries not to look as though she's looking. She tries not to fall so visibly asleep. She calculates how loudly she would have to scream for the neighbors to notice. Louder than their televisions and fucking. She practices grabbing the kitchen knife that she hides under her mattress. She gets up and puts the iron in the middle of the bedroom floor. She chuckles knowingly as she trips over the cord.

Vida Henderson

The Tree on Guillot Road

In my other life,
I killed a man,
a mud-colored man
who screamed blood.
I drank his musty sweat
and surrendering urine
as his legs cast dancing shadows
upon the dusty ground.
Salty eyes watched me,
but I did not break.
I held him tight.
I held him strong.
I held his life
inside the core of me
And felt it slip away
Into nothingness.
    Hanging there
    Like a wet rag
    On a clothesline.

Sean Hill

Uncle John

Uncle John was caught stealing a ham
from Mr. Ennis's Meat Market
when he was seventeen
(a cured ham)

Lost his taste for it
locked up
fourteen years

Ham salty and earth-red
sliced with the fat hanging on
yellow sunshine on a white plate
The hambone cut crosswise
rings marrow
a dark eye
All in the skillet
making gravy for grits

Lost the taste for all things salt
the ocean he hasn't seen
woman and man

He don't never want to see
no more ham on his plate
Hates pigs
Was hard for him
Hates white folks too

Time off for good behavior
They didn't hold him to the last six

He's a hog farmer
only eats beef and chicken and turkey
fish turtle and rabbit
squirrel possum and coon
and he seasons his greens with smoked oxtails

Can't raise white folks to slaughter.

Major Jackson

viii. Block Party
[for The Roots]
from *Urban Renewal*

Woofers stacked to pillars made a disco of a city-block.
Turn these rhymes down a notch and you can hear
the child in me reverb on that sidewalk where
a microphone mushroomed with a Caliban's cipher.
Those couplets could rock a party from here to Jamaica.
Its code was simple: *Prospero's a sucker-emcee.*
Smoke rising off a grill threatens to cloud all memory;
my only light, the mountainous cones of streetlamps.
Did not that summer crowd bounce in ceremonial fits?
Ah yes! It was the deejay, and his spinning TECHNICS
delicately needled a groove, something from James Brown's
FUNKY PRESIDENT. Then, working the cross-fade
like a light switch, he composed a stream of scratches,
riffs. Song broken down to a dream of song flows
from my pen; the measured freedom coming off this page
was his pillared spell of drums. It kept the peace.
A police car idled indifferently at the other end of the street.
What amount of love can express enough gratitude
for those reformulations, life ruptured then looped back,
def and gaudy like those *phat*, gold chains?
Keep to sampling language, keep it booming
like Caliban yelling, *Somebody! Anybody! Scream!*

Yvonne A. Jackson

Underwear

the girl we found pantiless
on the sandbox monkey bars,
she wouldn't come down.
we laughed
gawked up at her crease
but the bare-bottomed hussy
kept climbing
pantiless and proud
to the very top
her spread legs, girders
holding together
her steel mountain.
it was we who fell
tumbled into her living room
plunged into the smell of grease, rank
unwashed or barely washed
clothes, a father snoring
drunk, drawn shades
its windows, closed mouths.

she looked down at us
eyes hard as sand.
only then did she return
to her living room.
leave us children
to our play.
she didn't look back. we lost her
at the edge of the building
we making war among the dunes
we with panties
mothers
and lighted livingrooms.

Valerie Jean

Another Version

Eve never begged him to
eat it. She only bit at red
skin, and chewing, smiled.

He could not stand the way
the juice glistened on her
cheeks. He never thought

of his God, to ask or seek
for guidance from his fear.
Burning with an unfamiliar

quacking in his bones, he
only saw her lips, smacking
on forbidden fruit. Long

afterwards, snuggled under
the quilt of her heaving
body, his mind was still

stitched to the idea that she
had, somehow, betrayed him.
Soon as she fell into uneasy

sleep, he crept straight away
to that discarded core to devour
the soggy brown-edged remains.

He sucked in hard, swallowing
all the seeds. He became a wolf
with an appetite for her blood.

Brandon D. Johnson

Past Time

I zigzag sidewalks shunning land-mined gym-shoes
hear chanted anthems of long-dead rappers between
broken glass and chewing gum. buildings grow beards
before they'll collapse under secret acts now spilling from
windows. I don't look into darkness blessed with screams.
alleys howl death's miasma, and dead-eyed
men walk with babies' cries in their hands.

gold Timbs ask if I'm alright, but I know it's
not casual salutation, this test of sobriety. amusement
parks are three hours down the road, but this is a ride no one
can get off without a root, or a grinning gangster's passkey.

my woman's sitting in an empty hotel room, bulb giving life to shadows.
puppets made of hair and cardboard.
this is the night of *at lasts* and I'm not there to help her breathe.
candles and Cassandra fade, cheese hardens, crackers *don't* anymore
she's a decumbent Coke bottle crushing plush pile like the furniture
but I won't see a taxi's insides without a pale finger and a
smile I lost ten miles and a blister back.

I see Melle first, a man nasty as Blues songs sung for sassy women.
he's scrippin to his boys, standing round a fire, embers spiraling
past frost-bite like lightning bugs headed for the moon.
downtown phrases slide from his lips, hotrods on an icy road
a midnight cold as the hawk slipping under a girl's skirt.
last man tried to play Melle's game left a halfway house in shambles
him unable to reconcile shame and recovery.

men like us don't know when to shut up, so the jives
go lateral as footballs in a blooper reel, neither knowing
when to be bested or accept a coup de grâce gracefully.
daddies' reps are ground underfoot, mommas need to know
better than come into a hungry man's mind when he's scheming.
we dozen so hard family trees burn, shuffle and fall like
cards in the hands of a Times Square Monte artist. show your money
lose it fast. men like us don't know when to shut up.

the periphery catches shrapnel, a laughing crony's sister bites the
dust of innuendo. collateral damage. errant bombs nick the noses of
ne'er-do-wells and neighbors out to catch the spectacle before
the cops make rounds. barbed hands ease trade tools from
waistbands and sweat socks. Melle lifts a forty to wet
a worn tongue, quashes the rumble before damage is done.
when his eyes begin to float, *I'm gone.* I ease toward
the curb, a pair of tight jeans glowing at the edge of the fire
remind me of my heart's destination. a street lamp wobbles when I pass,
the light makes night look like a Harryhausen invention.

my woman's angry as a bull who's missed a toreador too many times.
chocolates soften on unsullied pillowcases. the hawk rattles
windows asking to be her lover. she snatches the *do not disturb* sign
maybe the bellman needs a new babe to escort. why lose black lace
and scalloped borders, to the cleaning lady. clock hands point the way out
she knows nothing's coming in before night ends its solitary shift.

Jacqueline Johnson

Bruised Fruit
(Pantoum—A variation)

Inspired by "To the Days" by Adrienne Rich

Some say we are tossed aside bruised fruit
flowers of a generation of men.
Blackened banana, brown exposed apple core.
Who would not know us or our beauty?

Flowers of a generation of men.
Scream of a million sway-back brown women.
Who would not know us or our beauty?
Our desires held chaste over abysmal hunger.

Scream of a million sway-back brown women.
Daughters of moonlight carry love's calabash on their head.
Our desires held chaste over abysmal hunger.
Life pulses in us like the knowing in Sula's blue eye.

Daughters of moonlight carry love's calabash on their head.
Some settle for being second and third wives.
Life pulses in us like the knowing in Sula's blue eye.
Loves' sweet water cannot parch a drought four centuries long.

Some settle for being second and third wives.
Daughters mothers, keepers of moonlight.
Loves' sweet water cannot parch a drought four centuries long.
Wizened women gather from palmeres to charleston.

Daughters mothers, keepers of moonlight.
Seeds our men sow in other villages undo us.
Wizened women gather from palmeres to charleston.
Forgotten, yet open fields of our future billow.

Seeds our men sow in other villages undo us.
We who own power of plums in full blossom, beckon.
Forgotten, yet open fields of our future billow.
Sounding of getupandkeepthe planet together women.

We who own power of plums in full blossom, beckon.
Blackened banana, brown exposed apple core.
Sounding of getupandkeepthe planet together women.
Some say we are tossed aside bruised fruit.

Karma Johnson

Cum. Cum, cum
cum the bustiered breasts entreat
cum, cum, come taste come
sample come try come
buy me I'm slick and
sticky as fly tape—gonna get you
stuck—come fuck this
pussy. All you got ta do
is sling the Benjees
and we can get down.

    i see this ho/on a red bed
    she on her knees
    her legs and ev'ything showin
    she kinda fat, got big eyes
    her hair real
        why do my mama say
        i don't need to look?
        it's just a ho picture—i known
        what that is since the first time
        i was in second grade
        besides—it's like the ho girl
        lookin at me, tellin me
        cum, cum on, you

Betta snatch yo eyes
off that mess/not for children.
Wouldn't do no white woman
singer like that, make her get buck naked like that
to sell a album. It's like they ain't even
makin records for music no more—just freak
video/phone sex wit a beat—
and they don't care who sees it.

Least put that shit up in the back of the store if
you hafta have it. Or somewhere you gotta ax for it—
not out here for my children to look at
comin out the Baskin Robbins. Know
they wouldn't put that shit up on they Madison Avenue.
Hold still and put on your goddamn hat!
    Sheeit, baby
    everybody wanna get blowed
    make somebody go low and mouth no
    apology. It's all about the ground right about now—
    who can crawl is who can make the money flow.
    I don't owe nobody nuthin/My picture—my face
    my titties—on every other block down 1.2.5/what?!
    I'm a muthafuckin icon—y'all don't know—it's just 2
    years I been off AFDC/now you tell me
    Babylon ain't fallin/I'm on every other block
    anywhere, block—it's a continuum
    block/every muthafuckin
block, I'm a symbol/it's a continuum
        block/driven by capital, black
it's a continuum, anywhere
block I'm on the black
   symbolic anywhere block
       black bitch I'm here
on the block, stood there
on the block, black, block
   stood there on the
block/picture
   stood there on the/auction
black, stop—stood there on the
stop/black—auction

stood there on the block
stop/now you tell me
Babylon ain't/driven by capital, black
on every muthafuckin
block

Patricia Johnson

In a Place Where

crepe myrtle hangs
brushes the ground
japanese beetles
ride each other's back
the leaf eaten away beneath them
hills and mountains
carve out the sky
random pieces in a rag quilt
queen annes' lace, ragweed
sweetpeas and joe-pye weed
choke the roadside
there are no signs stating:

wild flowers, do not pick

in a place where
crows big as cats
feed in fields dotted
with wagon-wheel hay bales
cattle, flies sipping
from their eyes
seek shade from trees
along the fence line
in a place where
you drink a breath and
hay, manure, magnolia
clover and wild primroses
ride the intake of air

a dirt road is swallowed by pines
smoke rises above silver maples
the smell of hog killing
hangs in the air
heavy shoes crunch gravel
down and up an incline
to the trailer
offset by trash
circled by weeds

on a mattress
in the front yard
crumpled and headless
a Black man burns

July 25, 1997; G.P. Johnson
was burned alive and decapitated
in rural Grayson County, Virginia
in a place where
I call home.

A. Van Jordan

The Journey of Henry "Box" Brown

Perhaps Henry Brown remembered Golgotha,
the taunt of the trail, the inevitable end—
the enviable end—the sting of vinegar doused eyes,
much like his own urine drenched skin, or
he remembered those who pined in bondage,
those who longed for the freedom of either his box,
the carpenter's geometric womb, the nails
pulled straight from hands to hold
the walls together till his new life,
or the voice, as if from above, in his head
which whispered, "Go and get a box,
and put yourself in it," that voice which dreamt
him through white hands, through bounds
his black face could not cross; first,
to the express office, the box placed on its end,
so he started with his head downwards—
as if he were on the verge of life—
the crate marked "This Side Up
With Care," but no one cared and no one
bent to break his falls or to stop the blood
from rushing to his temple—
two hours on his head, veins strained, eyes
bulged, death's breath held—
then, three o'clock in the morning, a depot,
now with the box directed right side up,
to the home of a friend in Philadelphia
whose trembling voice—imagine,
on the outside and *his* voice trembled—
asked, *Is all right within?* to which Henry,
in a trumpeted tone, replied, *All right.*

Henry Brown was a slave who mailed himself to freedom with the help of an abolitionist group in Philadelphia. He got the idea from a vision from God.

Douglas Kearney

Anansi Meets Peter Parker at the Taco Bell on Lexington

so i'm at the taco bell on lexington across the street from pizza hut & panda express. you know the one? i'm tryin to eat my sixty nine cent (times is hard) bean burrito when this cardigan wearin m.i.t. lookin muthafuckin shutterbug grubbin chilitos like a deep throatin flick chick clicks a pic of me.

                                            now, crazy ain't my way, figure fool on some ansel adams kick, could be snappin shots of fast food spots & other americana ka-ka for the *ny post* the *daily planet* or the *times*. so i ig him, rip the plastic packet of semi-salsa, spread red on the skid marked tortilla taco bell call bean burrito (times is hard) when *click:* mr. shutterbug has another private kind of kodak minute with me in it. i say "do i look like tyra banks? best slow your roll or i'll crop your shot but good!" he reach in his pocket & pass me a business card. hmmph. "*peter parker* with the *daily bugle*? never heard of you." six inch thick glasses mask his face but i know he a white boy when he say he doin "research on quaint & obscure local characters" all national geographical & shit. i wave six arms say "i look obscure to you muthafucka?" he do a no offense crawfish, say "i mean, i've never seen anyone with your style. i'll pay you if you let me take some more pictures" figure mr. pentax pack stacks of dinero & bean burritos (times is hard) ain't been tasty for awhile. & cash for a couple of shots— why not get over? so we step outside. i profile against the wall like the baller i was back in the day. tell him how i used to be a playa swingin hut to hut, chick to chick, friendliest daddy-long-stroke in the hood. he smile like it's all good, quit clickin pics, slip me two benjis, shake all my hands & he down the street before you could say chalupa.

two weeks later benji lookin more like abe & i'm back at the border orderin bean burritos (times is hard) when out the window i see some jackass in red & blue spandex swingin down lexington with some half-ass spider moves. next day the same clown get front page of the—*daily bugle*? hmmph. *spiderman.* got his own book, tv show, movie & everythang. ain't that a bitch. but i ain't bitter. ain't nothin new. i mean you saw what happened to that nigga b'rer rabbit after that bugs bunny shit. hmmph. couldn't be me cause see, it's like i told you: crazy ain't my way.

Anansi is the major trickster figure of the Ashanti and Akan. He alternately takes the form of a man or spider. Peter Parker is the secret identity of the American superhero, Spiderman.

Nzadi Keita

what does it take
(kudos to Junior Walker)

it is the summer of shing-a-ling and baby blue,
culottes and french twist.
you are in training for cute, a student
in the social arts,
measuring how well
your short nose
and heavy lips present
under a dim blue bulb.

slice your bangs with three fingers, practice
smiling. do something with those undainty hands.
chips and dip on a napkin—not *too* prissy.
make the drink last; let your eyes
climb the cup to the edge:

here come the fellas,
tumbling down linoleum steps
magnetic in pressed
white shirts and creamy sweaters.
beautifully foreign,
dark necks like spice jars, opened.
toothpicks winking and tilting
those half-smiles. dangerous veils;
who knows what they'll do.
test the tightness of your skirt;
will it **give** too much. on the **fast song**, browse;
flip the records. jiggle the butt to make up
what is lacking in your face.

on smokey, the fellas launch
from their dark harbor like a fleet of ships.
hack the frozen space in your throat; cute demands
a tongue unwrapped, a bright
sprinkle of remarks, a cache of candy.

tease your earrings, cool your eyes
while the fellas cruise. sit without sinking,
amused on the edge of the couch. no sorry
vibe to anyone. keep moving, dance a little
on your own in case
nobody taps your hand.

Janiece Kirton

Water dripping
leads her to dream
A familiar man
paddles a raft.
The evening calm
as the rocking waves
The Jersey shore
shifting further away
Already they have
gone past the rocks
The sound of the waves
is like cooing
The water rising
Over her feet
Rising over her knees
over her hips
There is no sound
that anyone can hear
to save her life
She twists off her head
It arrives
on a foreign shore.

Jacqueline Jones LaMon

white butterfly

> *over time...i've been building my castle of love...just for two...*
> *though you never knew you were my reason...*
> "Overjoyed," Stevie Wonder

    beyond lavender rosebush
    home to swarms of bees that never sting

    beyond yellow tulips
    strengthened against the narrowness of bed

    beyond magenta oleander
    blossoming beyond its confines

a haven

i sit on your porch
drink wine on your lawnchairs
recall a lifetime of conversation
conducted over *ebony* catalogues
and letters from new york sisterfriends

this is your house
you said
come home anytime

the radio plays
in your windchimes

i mouth your name
cling to steveland's melody
and watch a white butterfly
light on your chair

Sherry Quan Lee

Bruise Number Two
from *A Woman's Cycle*

Where are bruises hiding today? Not one interrupts my morning. I am not afraid.

Snow sifts through cold air. Winter is late this year.
The windshield of my 1996 black Ford Contour is clouded. Periodically I turn on my wipers to clear my vision. Mom, she never learned how to drive. Did she even want to? We carried groceries in a metal cart on wheels. It was fun when I was small, tagging along. Embarrassing when I was old enough to go each Saturday to the neighborhood store, six blocks from home, by myself. But still, I wanted to please Mom. (It didn't matter Dad disappeared with the car and the family pride.) I would find myself doing things I didn't want to do for thirty years. I thought Mom would eventually applaud. But I got clothes stuck in the wringer washer, laughed at jokes I didn't know were *dirty*, and wrote about marijuana and God both in the same essay.

Mom rode buses. Took yellow taxicabs when she had five dollars. Usually she walked. Walked straight ahead through Minnesota winters. Winter or summer, most of her life she was cold. Frozen. Frozen fingers frozen heart. She didn't know how or she didn't want to unbutton layers of synthetic clothes that swaddled her beauty. She never unzipped the fear that tied up her tongue.

I'm not certain where I'm traveling, and I've never had a new car to get there. But I sit on gray leather in my '96 Ford Contour limousine dreaming about how to get there. But I'm not cold. My hooded parka is crumpled in the back seat with empty cigarette boxes (I'm a crisis smoker) and faded maps. It is early morning. The sky is midnight black.

From one generation to another, colors change. I stop for dark brown mud-thick coffee, slightly burnt. And watch the sun rise through glass windows of a fast food restaurant. Eat a biscuit sausage sandwich just because I can. What did my Mother see locked in a house on a hill surrounded by chokecherry trees? Everyone I know wears glasses. Bifocals awaken my vision. I was taught not to look, touch, see. Writing has taught me what's important. Pay attention to detail. Observe. Reflect.

Most days, I practice what I preach. The days I write. The days surprise, awe, wonder—extend my rigid imagination. Images magnify in the reflection of my belief. Today it is snowing as if each tiny flake is on a serious mission. Doesn't even touch ground, but dances on a horizontal plane. When will gravity escape me? I want to float. Feathers are light, and graceful.

The snow moves like traffic, forward. Forward. Forward. Doesn't everyone have some place to go? And a reason for going there? Mother went to a one-room high rise. Old and opinionated people (mostly women) everywhere. Mom went to her room and locked her door. Sometimes I knocked. Once in awhile she answered. When she peeked through the pinhead sized glass hole she observed what offerings I brought. She responded most favorably to peanut butter kisses. Hershey Kisses, the most recent editions of Harlequin romance novels, and lottery tickets.

Where are you now, Mother? Are we at our house in South Scandinavian Minneapolis? Are we sitting on red vinyl chairs at a gray Formica table? Have you dunked your Zwieback toast in your cup of Hills Brothers Coffee? Has my gingersnap melted in my milk? Or are we older. You with yet another State Fair yardstick in your hand. Me crying. You swatting. Me screaming. It wasn't a game, Mother. I really didn't know why I was crying— or maybe I just didn't have the words to articulate my confusion. Or are we younger? Years one through four, lost like my Father to memory? I believe it's not too late to break the silence. What is it I should know? Did you love my Dad? Did he love you? Did either of you love me? Which hurt left you lonely?

White isn't a color, so why did I think it could cover your secrets? Four little Chinese/Black girl secrets and one little Chinese/Black boy secret. Yet, I must have believed your truth. Not that it would set us free, but that truth is beyond a young girl's imagination. Yet, snow has always fascinated me. Each snowflake different. Each flake so white, so bright— my black beauty glistened.

Ahh, the color black. Brilliant. Breath-taking. Beckoning.

I am awake to midnight black each morning. Embrace it. Get into my '96 black Contour Ford, headed on a black journey, down black roads, my mojo working. I am the black daughter waving to you, Mom. Put your hand in the air, and acknowledge me. I will see you because I'm searching, looking, paying attention.

After death do bruises disappear? The doctor said Mom had a *leukemia blast*. This after he and we all agreed leukemia wasn't what was killing her. Wasn't what would kill her? Black was the color Mother crushed. Or did it crush her? Her sisters dealt with Black in other ways—marrying it, cursing it, celebrating it, being it. However blue. Blue was Mother's sadness.

Mother, smile. I am an artist. I am mixing words on my palette. Creating. Purple is the woman I have become. I have not become you, Mother, as everyone had threatened or at least joked about. You have become me. And we are both stronger for it.

I am glad it snowed today. See, Mother. I am an angel sculpting in the snow. Cold and wet. Flappin' my wings. Flappin' my wings. We are flying.

Reginald Lockett

The Dumb Class

They didn't use
nice terms like
learning disabled to describe
us, the students in Miss Cortez's
basement classroom
at Longfellow Elementary
next to the storage rooms
where the janitors
kept big push brooms, mops
buckets,
and huge barrels
of industrial cleansers, soap,
and wax.

We
were just dumb, retarded,
or slow,
embarrassments to
brothers, sisters, and cousins
who disowned us
the second their feet
entered
the schoolyard gate.

I was the youngest at seven
and the only one
in the right grade.
The others were older,
like Carlene, fresh
from Arkansas,

who was twelve
in the third grade, dipped snuff,
and chewed tobacco;
Theodis, who was fourteen
in the fifth and kept
being held back because
he spent most of the year
locked up at juvenile hall;
and Billy Boo who was sixteen
in the sixth and wore a wavy process
teased into a big pompadour,
and had a ditty-bop walk.

That year,
while Miss Cortez read *Home and Garden*
and let the class run wild,
I taught myself to write in longhand
and how to do
third, fourth, and fifth grade arithmetic
after the colored school nurse
discovered I needed glasses,
a pair of glasses.

Doc Long

Rules for Cool
Book One

      1
become friends
with the color blue
      2
always serve music warm
with everything on it
      3
never say yes on Friday
or the first of the month
      4
check out peoples' games
from across the street
      5
only speak loud enough
so that spiders with shades on
can hear you
      6
always keep an extra pair of shades
to wear at night in the house
      7
dance, but act like you're not dancing
and when you do, always be cool and in your hump
      8
wear clothes that make you look like
one of those jazz dudes
      9
be into deep heavy stuff
and carry large intelligent words
around in the same pocket with your money
      10
only sing to your woman on weekends

devorah major

crops not harvested

ah, the mouth-watering fantasies i have had
about men i wanted to, but never did, love
(even if only for one night)

not ordinary green banana thoughts
but lush orange papaya dreams
rolling smooth black seeds off
the edges of my tongue

once my hands cradled a soft-furred kiwi
its delicate center inviting me to swallow it whole
another time it was the thin green shell of a mango
pulled aside to reveal undulating strands of saffron flesh
smooth and thick waiting to be bitten

one was a winter pear soft from steam
drizzled with honey and just a touch
of fresh ginger for some bite

and i still recall the pungent smell
of wild raspberries whose juices
threatened to burst over my fingertips
the minute they were touched

and oh that glistening plum
perfumed syrup seeping through
tart black skin

that grove of mulberry love
staining my lips and cheeks
that bowl full of honeydew wedges
resting between my thighs

ah, the orchards i have walked
the fruit i have relished
yet left on the vine
waiting for a better season

Dawn Lundy Martin

(F)

(A body wrapped
in a clean white sheet)

In the wrist's movement.

(Without thought)

In and out.

(Like Braille)

I whisper it again.
(F)
(And amass)

       Cut.

The nostrils keen, flared.

(Earth existing)

It is the first time.
(It again)
(Muffled and incomprehensible)

In and out.

She is the beginning of ritual.

In—in climb.

I watch it being itself.
As in water turning to steam.
(Or coal to dust)

Curled is the ear.
(Straining)
What? What?

Hurry —

      ssist

            finish.

Shara McCallum

In the Beginning

In the garden of dusk
the father is being born.
One part of his mind
crystallizing into salt,
clear and stinging as the sea.
One part unhinging
like the fruit of the tree
plucked too soon from its stem.
Here, he will learn to speak
in the voice of the Lord,
believe that sound
to be the echo of himself.
Here, he will perfect
the loneliness that,
in its brilliance,
like the sun, blocks
all others out.
Years later, night
falls in the garden,
falls across the leaves,
across the grass, leaving
a trail of silver light.
His daughter is born.
He does not know her face.

David S. Mills

Hide and Seek

Busted
With *Yeah-Yo* on some trumped
Up charges, way the fuck up

In *Buttfalo*—three-time loser—he was
Looking at lockdown

Or wearing a wire, fronting
Like he's still a foot

Soldier while documenting why
December flinches, why

When Bolo pisses shaved
Ice he leaves black

And blue marks on abandoned
Buildings. Bolo was who 5-0 wanted

To collar so my brother had to drop
Dime. At first he only picked up pennies

Of info: whispers, a shipment. He did
What 5-0 demanded, but they lied.

They didn't have a Witness
Protection Program. Now

He's got to break
Out under the cover

Of a star-filled night. He's got
To *swing* twinkle to twinkle.

So he calls and wants me to
Let him chill at my crib. How can he

Stay with me and Mamacita?
She's not up on how hot chocolate

Can get. She's never met the whites
Of Bolo's eyes, those garlic cloves

That blink and crack. "You're
Playahating Steve, I'm your baby

Brother, your blood. Remember
When we used to play 'Hide

And Seek?' I always told
You when Boonty was coming.

You owe me." "We already lost
Him and Dre to the virus.

Peanut, you're the only brother
I got left so there are one of two

Things you can get through
Your skull, this point I got to make

Or a hollow point: Bolo could track
You to my crib and do you,

ME and MY lady. NO
Family left!" "I feel you.

A'ight, wire me some cheddar
Cause I'm gonna have to outrun a gang

Of locusts and smoke, then
Plea-bargain with stray dogs

And sorcerers for my life."
"Peanut, I belong to Sunday. Jesus,

Roll and burn the sidewalks you run past
Like they're blunts or high school

Diplomas, then they'll be no prints
From your Timbs, no traces of you."

"You're buggin!" "Maybe. I don't know
 The rules of your universe

Anymore: the put up or shut up;
The Kango and do-rag; the low-income

Black holes where tomorrow and
Sunshine never escape; your days spent

Teetering on a shabby high
Wire between low-lifes and angels."

His pager goes off. "I'm holy
And I'm ghost, Steve, one love." Click.

I tried to say something but my tongue
Was a canoe, capsized and trembling,

Anchored in a dark tent
Of spit, I've decided

I ain't playing Hide
And Seek no more, no

Covering my eyes, no waiting
For my cell phone to scream,

No peering through the crack
Between my pinky and ring

Finger: Peekaboo the I.C.U.
Of Lincoln Hospital. Peanut's body

The horrible geography of a drive-
Bye bye. I can't look. See, my baby

Brother's problems have always had one thing
In common: him.

Veronica Mitchell

Mea Culpa

My cousin says that heroin makes him normal.
I think he means he's able to see
without the eyes of the divine.

He's given over to listening to whispers
of poppy seeds, spent 50 years watching
shadows write the hit lyric

and play the perfect chord change, seen
an idea's perfection, yet he's refused to dance
with the clumsiness of translation,

too paralyzed to imitate: take the purest then pour
in one's mind. But, he has perfected a chemistry,
a slight-of-hand that keeps death at bay:

He concocts speed balls, that cocaine-heroine cocktail,
an invisible worm that slips into the soul—part man,
part woman, a chorus of Glories.

Last May, his mother found him in a stupor, flat out
on the bathroom tile, her Lourdes-blessed rosary
across his chest: Mother, have mercy on me, again.

From the shadows before birth, did he watch her extend her arms
to a stranger and give over her infant girl? Did my cousin see
that in that exchange his mother would give over her life to him?

Lenard Duane Moore

On First Reading the Introduction to Natural Birth by Toi Derricotte

I sat there like an owl
on that narrow Cranbrook bed,

which reminded me
of my army bunk,

my other life
with the calling cadence

for sacred survival.
I was in that singing skin

twenty-two years
in front of now.

A man marching in/out
of his own life like a ghost,

I was on duty's time
searching for a woman

to join her grace,
her natural self.

I wanted to pluck loneliness
from someone's heart.

I practiced living
when hearing her speak

in the chambers
of my poems:

all over the barracks
the season of birthing

amidst the general orders
and the long days

through Fort Jackson
to Fort Eustis

to Stuttgart
and back home

where it came
to the creation,

always exploring
with my future wife:

falling, rising and falling
into the waterfall.

It was too sweet to stop,
to catch our breath.

Our concerto reached grace,
our natural selves.

We wore love like ribbons,
and we still do.

We are a whole continent,
beyond military borders.

I must tell this story
to our daughter

who is nearing nineteen,
the same age my wife gave birth:

and from the fort,
it was a natural one.

Renée K. Moore

Eurydice

Must have said something
more than *farewell*
It wasn't reluctance
more using her legs
and feet on something
that didn't give
The asp's teeth
left her ankle grey, purple, tender

Not hearing her uneven steps
his eyes on darkness fading to light
his mind oblivious to the power in his voice
in his fingers coaxing
curved wood and taut string
So much Heaven in his hands
all Hell stopped to hear

His thoughts
small questions smothering
what always had been
what came with melodies
born of his fingers
baptized in his throat

He forgets a god is a god
Forgets to let her scent confirm divine darkness
She sees him turn from the light
sees his charms become vapor
and send her back to Hades.

Tracie Morris

Combinations

The cylinder, bolt, chain, bar
fixed from inside
on the 9th floor out of 18.

The second wing out of three,
The sixth building of fifteen.

Terraces fenced floor to ceiling.
Little squares grid Sergio
Valentis, the forearms

Gina and Marvin kissing at twilight
folded, shifting like playing cards.

Harryette Mullen

The Fire This Time

Cave Canem
A poet's retreat
A safe house
A poet's sanctuary

Cave Canem
The poets are dreaming
When a loud noise wakes us
I grab my words and run

Cave Canem
A dog is barking
A fire is starting
The poets are awakened

Cave Canem
The fire is spreading
Detroit's ears are burning
The poets are wide awake

Second Annual Cave Canem Occasion Poem

Mendi Lewis Obadike

Tell me this is because we remember long

> The South, Africa, and 'blackness'—are our mythical beginnings and our articulations of the mythologized connections...Community is more easily said than encountered; we hear different calls on it.
> Wahneema Lubiano

We are in Santiago, in La Zurza. You look pure Atlanta. Mine.
Not just your skin and hair, also the borrowed baggy tee, the
Morehouse cap, crooked in the middle—a gift.

I want this to be black: You thank me for a favor. I answer:
"Para servirle." You tell me: "You sound Dominican. Americans say:
It's nothing. You say: *To serve you,* like us."

Your sandy voice, rubbing against itself, is home. But what of this?
"A la orden." "Para servirle." You hear your routes in my soil.
I have a foot-washing Baptist's mouth. Your speak is a seed in it.

Tell me our foremothers chose this way, this humbling
Of self before sister. Tell me history does not shackle
Our tongues and this rite is older than chains.

Gregory Pardlo

Pyro

It resisted extinction
on winter's tongue of earth
because, so long house-bound,
it burned to move. I felt for it
the way Michelangelo felt
for the figure trapped in stone.
On the six o'clock, I am the one gesturing,
heroic to be caught
on camera dancing behind the reporter,
now proud to see
myself transformed
into light, my celebrity
like flint agitating emery
tongues of the envious.
Paparazzi of broken glass
on asphalt mirrored wet and jugular
with hose. Homeless, drunks
and the otherwise extraneous
witness the pomp of flame
persistent as graffiti.
Huddled like hostages
behind a yellow tape,
my audience shivering tiny plumes
into thin air as the critics pimp
wet canvas up the engine ladder
into that burning house.
O to make a wick of myself,
the hot stone in my gut threatening
to ignite up the length of my spine,
rattling my glottis like the lid
on a boiling pot.

Tap water sounds like a fuse.
Strikes the basin and sparks.
Steam rises from what's burnt away
on the occasion of a kindling,
making a child of destruction
dutifully wash hands
of the sooty ruined thing.
Now they're showing
when the structure began to kneel;
reverent, infantile, innocent, reborn,
revealing timbers like one coming
out of his skin and embers litter the sky
raining hell suspended in the dingy exhaust
of one failed step toward the animate.
Housebound now I
think of joining the swarming,
sifting through all of them,
those glinting wind chimes wincing
at the sigh of my arrival, to reside
aloft like woodsmoke in the night.

Carlo Paul

The poem on your door

I.

is my final offering to you,
with genuine images of love
and thick words
like happy and forever

that hangs as a martyr—
the arms and feet of the paper
pinned to the wood seeking forgiveness
yet, what a calm response and omen:

your door locked tight;
our blunt similes
thinking they were
sledgehammers

II.

the poem on my door
was taken down late that evening
and after three days
it was framed and on my wall

where it hangs as a symbol—
to remember the days we were so lost
that your ink became lamb's blood on my door

Hermine Pinson

Redemption Song
to Estella Conwill Majozo

o sweet jesus, forgive our sins
save us from the fires of hell

if I contemplate myself
who will I bring forth
you
were
in my first dream
sitting

in the metaphysical chair
telling me
to believe in healing
and God's love
because I told you I was falling
like acid rain
falling

you gave me fatima's prayer as talisman
to keep between me
and narcissus prayer:

nobody's fall but mine
nobody's fall but mine
if I die and my soul be lost
nobody's fall but mine

I've hidden under the pillow
braking daylight
five more minutes
five more minutes

my father was a late bloomer
he says it's in the blood how
one child grow up to be

I call you mary sometimes
in our time
queen of hearts
who culls olive plants
who calls gaius
the folk

with clean eyes
holy mouth
you know how hush
tastes on the tongue
the quiet after vespers
or grace telling her beads

II
heed these things, you say
and none of my chicken little alarms:

"polish your glasses
breathe
drink more water
look where you're going
stop playing near the tracks
can undo you
the bump and grind
of wheezing trains
on tracks"

and nothing bites through
to the bone like
good intentions
are amateur fishermen
with big fish snapping
the string again

I won't lie to you
I still dream of trains
and tracks the bump and clack
of longing for distances
the soul can travel
all belongings stowed
or left long time ago

I pray for safe passage:

among
hollers and hoots
hollows and haints
squat by my neighbor's doorpost
with an orange mouth and a pumpkin
for fraternity

III
our father which art
our mother which art
our fish which art
snapping strings
kingdoms with no countryside
it all goes by so fast
when you're riding

daddy was a surgeon
he liked to say
I have had my fun
if I don't get well
no mo

which is safer, dad
bowing to the decrees of commissars
of the colon
which might also be a period
because that's the end, you know
which is a whole thing all to nother
maybe not cancerous after all
but all to nother
just the same

I have had my fun
if I don't get well
no mo

in all seriousness
introspective absolutionists
when in doubt they
the commissars
turn to surgeon fathers who recommend
immediate amputation of the poisoned part
and pride themselves on leaving no keloids

while the metaphysical part
leaks cleaning fluid

I have had my fun if I don't
get well no mo

I get anxious
with only the consolation
of remembering to breathe
in time
1-2-3-4-5-4-3-2-1
quarter notes
toward something saner

I got the ocd's
wanting to live can be
obsessive-compulsive
you know
can make you back up to the source
when the door's dust
reporting in
to gravestones with grass fingers
and no ears

estella,
your advice has proven to be cryptic:
"when singing things back together note stitches
breath where what can you do punchinella-punchinella
waits in patent leather shoes next to notebooks,
crochet needles, hypodermic needles, hospital gowns,
cigarettes, car keys, sunlight

mothers stand guard
on shotgun porches
biggers'-colored infinity ritual
they hold worlds
lead all souls to heaven

memory makes do
with changing time signatures
and compensation counts"
or not
since

1-2-3-4-5-4-3-2-1-2-3-4-5-4-3-

when the train thumps down the track
we can't sleep
clattering window panes and stew pots
sing back

I had a mother who could pray
I had a mother who could pray
if I die and my soul be lost
nobody's fall but mine

Cherise A. Pollard

Call and Response
for Myron

He comes to the window, all smiles,
pushes his prison issue glasses back on the bridge of his nose,
says, so excitedly, *Thank you for coming. Thank god, you're here.
Oh, God is good,* and we respond *all the time* knowing

he has been inside for three years without a single visit,
three years without trial but his trials are multiple: his mother died
when he was a child, his brother incarcerated,
his father refuses to respond to his letters, or to accept his calls.

We say, *And all the time,*
and he says, *God is Good.*

He carries a Bible, worn, the Gideon green fading fast
from hard prayer, pulls it out of his pocket, invites us to share
the sweet word. He reads passages of hope, and grace
through the stainless steel microphone. He's a ministry of one:

We need not worry, God will provide, wait on the Lord.
We sing *The road is rough, and the going is tough,
and the hills are hard to climb, I started out,
a long time ago, there's no doubt in my mind...*

Together we say, *God is Good
All the time...*

Ro-Lyan Reid

This Hour, When I Am Minute

floating above the earth
wrapped in the coarse tanglings
of imagination.

It's been several hours
since she left me
trembling still
and I have been like the wind
whispering down the outstretched tongues
of avenue and boulevard,
filling paper bags
with invisible substance,
picking up brown and yellowing leaves
putting them down
in different places.

I have crept through the spaces
between buildings,
whisked down alleyways
caressing the face of every vague beggar
like angel in disguise,
past the city's vacant corners
painted moods of amber
by streetlamps
like artistic vandals.

I have dreamed of us
making love
in cold weather
that made us
pull closer to truth
buried in one another's
bones,
I hold tightly to the imagined fragrance
of our labor,
the scent of her hair,
and thus the sandman
is cheated
during these sleepless
dreaming hours
though I am certain
sense will come of it.

Millicent Rucker

New Year's Eve

she tiptoes past
the grand mother lodge
spike heels hugging
blowfish feet
electric slide into
neon night shade
crows feet squint

ponderous legs
asynchronously hip
hope ing
two generations removed tunes
in midnight mayhem
she grooves
toasts and
taunts the fullness of time

Tim Seibles

The Further Adventures of Tutor the Turtle

> *Treasent-treasent Treezle-troam*
> *Time for this one to come home...*

After all I have told you, Tutah,
are you sure you want to be **black** in America?

> Well, gee, Mr. Wizard, times have changed.
> It might be a little tough, but I'll be down
> with the brothers—they'll show me the ropes.

But, Tutah, look—the Republicans are on the rampage,
white people, in general, seem like dangerous playmates,
and the black community is riddled with...with
self-inflicted wounds!

> Yet and still, Mr. Wizard, I would be African-American.
> I've read about Fanny-Lou Hamer and Malcolm.
> Black people are bold and resilient and I wanna **be** one.

> I wanna raise up like Michael Jordan and blow jazz
> with Wynton Marsalis and   and...

What, Tutah, what!!?

> And I *wants ta get funked up,* Mr. Wizard—*P-funk: The BOMB!*

Alright, Tutah, remember *if you hear any noise*
it's just me and the boyz:

{the incantation}

Two parts laugh and three parts pain
Cutting lash and hard-won gain

Thumpin' bass and rumble drums
Dr. King and drive-by guns

Skin of dark and spark of eye
Ella's grace and Pippen's glide

Purple Heart and might of back
Time for Tutor to be BLACK!

{Tutor, transformed, disappears into America.   Ten minutes pass.}

HELP, MR. WIZARD!!!

Nancy Mebane Shakir

Ancestors

The train thunders,
bringing memory
I am powerless.
Odor, hot and metallic,
blue-gray electricity,
scream of clashing metal,
plows into,
splits my forehead,
roars through my brain.

    I see them
Nancy Hunter, slave-cook
Big-boned, tall,
garbed in floor length apron every day.
Pride in her only born free
thin, black baby, Emma.

    Car after car
George Mebane, gentle, easy, pecan giant
fleeing to New Jersey from Civil War hunger,
the burnings and killings of Alamance County.
Swearing he'd eat anything that didn't eat him,
that he'd never go back to North Carolina.

    Row on row
Mozella Ray's Chickasaw mother,
refusing to ever sleep inside
a white man's house.
Living in her lean-to in the woods.

Blur of passengers
Pauline Hatwood, child of rejection,
eaten dead by cancer.
A too short life,
full with anger and sacrifice.

Looking neither right, nor left.
Widened sightless eyes.
Closed faces.
Every shade of earth,
Loam and clay and sand.

I weep.
Mute,
all speak to me in their silence,
testifying their lives.
Commanding me.
Saying,
"Remember me."
"Remember me."
"Remember me."

Evie Shockley

apprenticeship

bind yourself to us for a term of years,
and we will teach you something about
the business of living, they promised,

the hairs on my head, the ungolden
crown, the thick brown fern burgeoning
from the pot of my skull. so i did: took

a handful of my feathers, felt the down,
the barbed wire: squeezed the hair
into a ball: watched it spring open

and continue to unfold like a little life
released from the shell of my fist.
with all the permed possibilities of silk

snipped away, i learned that chemicals
don't free you for flight: that floating
is not being *in* a cloud, but in *being*

one, as light as fire rising into smoke.
tracing the circuitous route of one
strand, i came to understand that not

being direct is not to be without direction:
that looking around and around me
is how i grow. trust me, its curve confirmed:

spirals don't end up where they started.
and over the years, as the strands
banded together in groups, i learned patience,

felt the strength in numbers, solid yet
pliable, beneath the pressure of my palms.
i discovered the difference between locked

and locked in. now, my fingers snake
among the thickets on my scalp, searching
for the spaces that separate sections,

perpetually teased by tangles, reading:
that you can't cling to everything at once:
that some choices you make and some

are made for you: that the sweet sorrow
of parting is how you keep freedom
free, the recurrent work of a lifetime.

giovanni singleton

emerald

spinning wheel fortune. stagger the root.

warrior rifts. a cataclysmic sight. mythical

weave of bowed heads. discontinuous dreams

and drafts. drawing hands. acoustic bass.

plucked upright. mercurial conjure. strings.

such tongues ever leaning as in revelation.

Mistinguette Smith

Brunette

> "In Haitian folklore, when a star falls out of the sky, it means someone will die"
> — Edwidge Danticat

The tin roof rusts
onto my face all night.

The children sleep
like corpses. Even death

makes no sound here
passing house to house.

Hair iron red
your children smell like hunger,

lay close as spoons
for comfort. I dream

crossings, dark and
Atlantic. Metal

groans each time our
single bed frame shifts;

Dómi you call
as if to a child

afraid of darkness
and I am. Outside

there is no moonlight
just a bowl of shooting stars

spilled over head.
I count each one

that drops its dust
upon my face, traveling.

Christina Springer

Behind His Back, I Call Him Sambo
(excerpt from *The Splooge Factory Suite*)

a.
the first time he called, he wanted
to know if we accept Black clients.

of course. we are an equal
opportunity splooge factory.

do we have a blonde
to dominate him.

redhead, blonde, blue,
black brunette.

whatever. i smack
gum in his ear.

b.
when he shuffles in
i appraise him. as if

being a sister gives me the right
to criticize his fantasies.

that's the problem with Black
women. always using

men's minds like trampolines.

c.
that's why he comes here
to see white women.

they don't judge him.
the next time he wants

the blonde to call him nigger.
okay, but, racism costs extra.

d.
cathy must say nigger like she means it.
after seven weekly visits, he wants
only her. But, this time she must piss on him
as she screams nigger, riding crops his back.

at this point, I give him a web-address
for the KKK. It won't cost $200. He'll save

some money. Maybe get off.

Imani Tolliver

smoke

i miss the soft

tearing

with teeth

the silver ribbon

the wood burn

easy,

it is so easy to smoke

i miss choosing lighter and cigarette case

miss the hot, amber tip

of the slow drag

movie star and artist

suffer, i

dramatic, poetic

the inhale

feel the gas at the back

of my throat

the cloud in my lungs

the short travel of

the sad, sepia quotation

around important words

between kisses,

with hard liquor

my favorite song

smoke takes

took my father's life

took his sister's

took my teacher's papa too

she told me

after smelling the cough on my skin

smoking is less about

the abbreviation of breath

less about pretending

to be kerouac or dietrich

less about the clichéd sufferer,

survivor, etcetera

behind the poisonous cloud

i am protected from good-bye

see nobody smokes in la

at least nobody on my boho block

we yoga and gobble squares of tofu

happiest when we abandon the

chicken leg for basmati and curried eggplant

so the gaseous coat i wore

protected me from these healthy people

protected me from taking a chance

from say

kissing some brown boy

taking me home

getting my heart broke

don't nobody smoke in this town

get it

so safe i'd be with my rods of tobacco

sucking my own tomorrows

as my lungs got heavy

with tar and poison

i knew it was wrong

i don't smoke anymore

i like kisses and spare change

look at the pink of my lower lip

smell my shoulders, fingertips

clean, all clean

i don't miss the prickle of nicotine,

morphine of liquor stores

the heavy drugged drip

of the first puff

don't miss the expense

the drama

or the art of it

i miss the wall

the white cloak

the chiaroscuro tobacco brings

no one can find me when

my mouth is lit

isn't it awful how easy hiding is

tip to lip

strike

light

then blow suitors out of my mouth

funny how tears

make no dent in clouds

so here i am

smoke free

i don't even light incense anymore

now i smile real easy

not ashamed of a stain

or something falling out of my purse

it's just that sometimes

when a beautiful he

handles my heart roughly

when screaming into a phone is not enough

when tears give no satisfaction

sometimes i miss

the soft, acidic illusion of

"i got it all together

look at me, daring death"

    playing the foolhardy roulette of keep away

    keep away

Lyrae Van Clief-Stefanon

For My Husband's First Love

In pictures I spot you both quickly:
my husband, unmistakable
in the same plaid hand-me-down shirt
he wore for three years
of elementary school class photo days,
smiles, eyes on the camera
but attention focused
on you—your thick red hair
grows longer and longer
as you move with him
from classroom to classroom,
from third grade to fourth to fifth.

You are beautiful, a hint
of breasts beneath oversized sweaters
and the permanent shrug
of your eyebrows and shoulders
as if the camera probed, posed
questions and you wanted to hide
what you knew. I recognize
and love the boy who murmured
for hours when you phoned him, your voice
thin as the raised wakes
of a razor's welts across your wrists.

I imagine you cradling the receiver
against the side of your face
with your updrawn shoulder, your throat drawn.
I study each picture and wonder

how much your girlhood mirrored mine,
whether you dreamed of blankets
that hid, sheltered like force-shields,
the way I did. I was ten years old,
my husband says. In those years
when boys shunned girls on playgrounds
or teased them at the swings,
he wrapped love around you
warm and thick, invisible as faith.

You ran away from home
before you ever made junior high,
before you ever got to wear
his football jacket, something magic
into which you could disappear,
a safe place. You taught him
love is sanctuary, a haven he offers
daily. He grew into the man
he was becoming for you.

Karen Wade

When the Wind Blew the Door Open

Two little girls—three years apart
born to a red-dressed flirt of a woman
      an impotent father who loved them
Mother dressed them like twins
in plaid shirtwaist dresses
though one was stocky the other meek
They built unforgiving brick shelters
to protect against floods and droughts
Father flushed their lives with
Kentucky Gentleman
Mother protected herself against dry spells
coiled with another man
No one expected the twister
that tore off the roof
left smells of the mildew and ruin
Left two little girls
lightning struck
holding each other

Jay Ward

An Untitled Fugue

> Street walking silence
> steps between conversation
> like wind thrown sand
> through brownstone canyons.
> Brooklyn alleys
> always have something to say.

Flicked lighters cough rolled tobacco
piercing images
fluorescent basements
memory forgotten drama
like theater school.

> Gorges of stones left un-turn
> heavy like footprints that
> glide without laughter—
> the dismal moods.

Rudely awake
in the plane of two thoughts
them, us and the other stuff:
> orange glove left, on steps down to the train…
> white van driving, lights turned out…
> and green temples hidden on far sides of mountains…

>> Last time I talked to my man
>> night faced east
>> and Fela played in front.
>> Couldn't hear shit,
>> just lift weights
>> sunset on the back horizon
>> revealing forward shadows of Rumi and Shams.

Breathing Spirit…the spirit
       like the quickening of twilight stars
       —only one God
and happy to be blessed
       to be one with

             date trees swayin'
             wives waitin'
             and the kids wantin' to go to bed.
             "Hunter, Daddy's coming"
                    Man, I miss him like meals between fasts.
                    Forgot I had to eat, I am so close.

Sacrifice!!! means Sacrifice!!!
and true salvation will come to the soul.
"So let's get started…………what we came in the
room………………to do"

Afaa M. Weaver

Composition for White Critics Who Think African-American Poets Cannot Work in Contexts of Pure Concerns for Language and Post-PostModern Twentyfirst Century Inventiveness in Lyric Expression Due to Their Self-Limiting Concerns With Language as a Means of Self-Expression and Racial/Cultural Identity in Poetry that is Ultimately Perhaps Beautiful However Too Trite and Too Folksy to Be Post [II] Theorist Efficacy

for Jorie Graham

In lap tops on commuter flights, prop jets and peanuts
            with soda,

considering the last fate of this turning in the gyre, turning, turning
down the withering task of tunnels of white rabbits with watches
like flavo-flav, get out of here flavo flav blues ripping over the precipice
of an amanuensis turning into an insect crab creeping into the crescendo
of hollering arias in Verdi's Porgy & Bess,
            I see you now.

It is time for coffee.
                  Give me the complexity of knowing,
the gratitude of waking and wondering which window to thank for apples
in the window, becoming more red, redder than candy apple red,

a cosmic significance of not ever having a childhood and realizing how such
burdens as being less than an adult require the synthesis of forms,
of flow charts   of Lotus spreadsheets,
a sexual arrangement in Tibet.   I greet you now,
after this long trek to this point, this grove of pointed hedges where all time
changes and you gain or you lose or you understand there is no death,
only a perception of what it means to not breathe, this timeliness
of looking back some four hundred years and figuring the power of being able
                                   to tell some gross lie and call it history,
hoping the profit will land you a patio overlooking some wave crashing in
on a commercial for the Caribbean.
                      Metal lands in the crevice of cradles.

What matters is this waving, weaving of textures of night sky floating over
the stars, as in a night before a day of raining when you can look out and see
the gloom to fall on all you had hoped to do, accomplishing little, as who
will ever know we were here if everyone falls asleep at the machine,
just before the self-conscious narrative awakens and slaps your grandma
into some bootleg distillery during the casting/cattle and you awaken
understanding nothing except thighs on the throne in the basement,
the admonition fathers give you of being kind to the dumb poor,
as the poor are all dumb—

Listen, it's Falstaff running
in the accounting. What now, Caliban, in your old Chevrolet Impala, leaping
over the Wall Street disclosures and closures over any hope you ever had
of ascending to the lyceum of tootsie rolls, washing the hands of your dreams
in bleach and dishwashing liquid, oh what could be more tragic than dirty

beans and rice, the melting of the sauce turning to some letting out of blood,
away from the necessary folk richness of fables, Pitchy Patch Man
running alongside Cuchulain,

Kingston in the lurches, busy Mennonite women making shoofly pie
in the afternoon windows, in black arrangements, some Haitian cherub
peeping in through the gesticulating head of graffiti on the walls,
cross, criss cross, cross bronx expressway, the way you wear
your clothes backwards, dirt in the bloody beans and rice,
& from the Isles,

                                        screech Charlie Parker, screech,
screech and in the cruelest month take tea with the man in green makeup,
leaning over the bank ledge to creditors and robbers.

In a negro bar, the negro says
"Aren't we all Sicilians here?" & we must get home by seven

as Elaine and Bobbie must get to their archery lessons, and the dogs
must get their shots, and the utility vehicle needs another manicure,
in the shadows of the lilacs in the last door—ohdear, did we

thaw the roast—

on the train up the Mississippi to some distant point, a fading spot
in the darkening window where we will be held forever and forever,
tasting the harvest of tea leaves handed to us one day at a time,
with slices of banana bread, reading Trollope, oh god the torture
of details in British.

"I want to know,"

said some minister arraigned before God on a Tuesday when
every available angelic public defender was out somewhere being
laid, out in the sun, so close and not melting, as we watch the butter
churn in the bowl and melt for homemade pound cake, having heard
the announcement about the end of downtowns, now centers
with no cartography, and we add raisins, peeping into the bowl,
ready to put it in the mixmaster to swirl along with the flour.

"I can't imagine a world without me,"

said the reader in the reading room, safely ensconced in words
that are capable at any time of absolute and murderous rebellion,

leaping off the shelves, abandoning syntax and punctuation,
leaving off sound to become "Now, Tommy, stop stabbing the dog"
bigger than "V" destroyed the planet we wasted before they threw
us here to Earth the virtual entertainment, chewing Big Red.
                              Anyone for Big Red?

The first four notes
of Dizzy's Blues, please,
in the software,   *message returned to archives*
                              your mailbox is empty

The first four notes
of Dizzy's Blues, please,
random play this time
      this
         time

One   Two   Three   Four

America oh my poetry America
Fade to palm trees in Los Angeles

4/4 time   wide angle
sweet fire bird suite

That's the Wrap, Boys. Let's call it a movie.

Marvin K. White

Jitter

you wrong
and
you know you wrong
rollin up in here
like this the last place
you wanna be
like this the last stop
some train yard
comin up in here
liquor convinced
that puttin that hot sweet breath
all up in my ear
baby babyin me
you gon get
to put that ole rusty quarter
up in my jukebox
nigga you crazy
thinkin my underwear
just shimmy for you
cuz now you ready
to dance wit me
and this is where you take me
when i ask you
beg you
to take me out
you call this a ballroom
        say aint it just like sweets downtown
        say aint it just like jimmies on fridays
        say aint it just like the starlight
        say yo fast cousin bessie lee's basement
        say baby dont you love this courvoisier moon

and your bustin through window fist
brushin my cheek
and the carry the weight of the world
knot in your shoulders
and my backs small
big enough
your days hard worked calloused hands
to support the dip
you always surprise me wit
takin me back to bed
forgettin my prayers again
forgettin all the fast songs
forgettin you wrong
and you know
you wrong

Carolyn Beard Whitlow

Local Call

You handle me like I'm a local call.
I'm expensive. Long distance? Although
having never been loved I don't know how

to tell you so. So I answer the phone,
anticipate its diamond ring and let
you handle me like I'm a local call,

your line old as an old simile, stale
as a dead metaphor, you who's always had,
having. Never been loved, I don't know how

not to wish you would not stop stop not
loving me, the sidewalk running past me,
you handle me like I'm a local, call,

laugh in another language, hung phone screaming,
me unsure whether my anger volcano or match?
I don't know, having never been loved, how

to love, my mind stalled with graffiti,
imagination sore, hum "don't want nobody
don't want me," accept your local call,
having never been loved, knowing I don't know how.

angela williams

What Words?
for all us colored-eyed girls

What did that colored-eyed girl really know?
What did she see through those prisms she called eyes?

Was her life spinning on wheels of ever changing hues
    faster & faster — higher & higher?
Did her mother tell her something in private
              that stole her out the
                      monotony?

Did she say something like:
   Don't be afraid, girl, don't you ever be afraid
   To be happy—to be mad—to be sensible—to be senseless.
Did she take her aside, hug her real tight squeezing a life into her, and
                                                     whisper:

   Keep calm if you may, chile, but it won't be easy.
   I'm telling ya, it won't ever be easy.

Was it words that set her soul-house on fire
    higher & higher — burning & burning?
Was it words that nestled themselves into prisms, into wheels she called
                                                                                eyes?
Was it fire shut up in her bones that colored & colored again her life into rising
                                                              bursts of
                                                                             passion?

Were there words like *I love you* or words like *He loves me, loves me for real*?
Can words work miracles in their
                          promisings?
Can words usher in the flames never yet
                                    experienced?
Can words become the eyes of one colored-eyed girl
    and rock her senseless sometimes
    and rock her sleeping other times
    and rock her & rock her & rock her
                        all the time?

Can words calm her only?
What words of a mother, of a lover, of a father,
    of you, of me, of a colored-eyed girl can do more than they say?

What words did they tell you those colored-eyes spoke
  when it was over,
    when her wheels stopped spinning,
      when her soul-house converted
         into ashes
           into her soul-house converted
         into ashes
           into embers?

Did they say *I waited*?
Did they say *I longed for more*?
Or did they say *I loved & I loved & I loved*
      & I loved?

What did they say about what she did?
What did they say about how she lived?

Karen Williams

Offerings

> Your entrances and exits always leave something behind.

This be my sacrifice
This be my tongue ripped out
This be my burn baby burn
This be Holy Ghost fire shut up in my bones

This be my scream in a crowded theater
This be my jackrabbit running through the woods
This be project babies ducking blood and bullets
This be the ancestors gone on home

This be my power prophetic poem
This be my betcha a dollah though I am saved I can flow
This be my Uncle Tom Deadwood Dick shoot 'em up
This be the glory birth of my nation
This be my Soul Brother Number One
This be my talking loud and saying something

This be my slave ship my cotton patch
This be my residue of being plucky
This be my look y'all, I'm switching poem
This be my hips rising like moons and corn cake

This be fat babies bounced on knees
This be my pulling fluff out of toy poodles
This be my platforms or wedgies shoes
    whatever shoes were out in the 70s
This be my stint at being Jessica Care Moore
The Statue of Liberty in my dreams

This be my uptown boogaloo Motown poem
This be my invitation to think and dream
This be my throat clearing   hawking up
This be a fresh line from tight old poem
This be my moment to testify
This be my Wednesday night service testimony
This be understanding to have a testimony we must first pass the test

This be my confidence poem
This be my birdie and hook shot
This be my Jesus dying on the cross
This be his getting up on the third day
This be the best kind of ascension not quite like Maxwell's

This be my funky feel good poem
This be my chasing the devil poem
This be my checking the sky for rainbows poem
This be peace and love and all of God's blessings
This be my gift to you.

Lorelei Williams

Domestic

Each week a different woman
washes her smile in lemon
and soaks her eyes in bleach
scrubs her hands with heaven
and wipes the blood on her sleeves

dries her blues in the oven
plants her tongue in concrete
mops her face with semen
and waxes the floor with her teeth

wrings her womb into rosettes
irons her skin into pleats
vacuums the bones in the closet
and hangs her legs in the breeze

Shannon Williams

Leaves

...fall rainlike around me
I step through them, remember
ur lips on my cheek

Treasure Williams

Bull Dagger
an elegy for Brenda Delaine

the rumor was…
it had happened to you at nursing school
but my grandmama said
your whole family was "funny."

your brothers, shirelle and june,
with their conspicuously feminine
names
were the most articulate men
in our small southern sphere.

they talked proper
knew about wine
and read the black poets.

my mama, unfulfilled
and frustrated artist that she was,
would go next door and drink
with them.
have loud shit talking arguments about
nancy wilson and
jesse jackson's
affair,
and all that diana ross scandal.
it was '77, and I lived next door to
2 sissies
and
a bull dagger

Brenda Delaine
had lips
dyed charcoal
by pall mall's with no filter
she had cut her "good" hair short.
in the evenings,
I would jut my six-year-old knees
out of the back screen door,
sit on the low porch,
and scratch the hard dust
beside me with sticks.

Brenda Delaine was there
smoking quietly,
people watching.

sometimes,
a pretty high yellow woman
would come out too.
ask me about school,
if I had a boy friend,
what did santa claus bring me.

mostly,
we would look at the street in front of us,
speak to miss virginia
who never spoke back
and often
turned her head
as far left as it could go
so as not to look our way.

Bakar Wilson

Dream Cognition

The First Night

Grandma,
I saw you
Tearing out of your house
As if you saw demons.
You haven't walked
In two years.
I saw you run,
Stubby arms pumping
Like you were running
The last leg of a race.
You were a tornado
Crossing the street,
Coming towards me.
I ran into my house
To take cover.

The Second Night

You tried to break up a fight
Between your cheetah and a lion.
I held you back as they tumbled
Into your bedroom
Promising to have
The other's blood.
You ran in after them.
I followed.

Your cheetah,
On the floor,
Licking his lips,
While the lion lay dead
On your bed.

The Third Night

I am awake in Nashville
Waiting on a phone call
Wondering if you destroyed death
Again.

Ronaldo Wilson

Two Sequences from *The Urticaria Series*

4. *viscera*

when my father attempts to convince the dirt monger
about the misplaced top soil

four yards are in the wrong place
and two are mixed in the compost

your men will use it   will sell it the dirt monger argues
you get no more

my father responds
i am looking at the dirt right now
it is wrong   i have a receipt

the dirt monger says he sees the trees
outside his office   the parking lot

his baby screams from the garbage
his life is blown apart by waco
his life is an explosion
his life is full of fear
he's fed up   *i don't care*
he says and hangs up

in a dream my father is dying in the kitchen
then dead and died with his throat full

of logic stuttering and choking on it

5. *example as anaphora*

my father is driving us home
when the cop shoots his brights into
the back of our pinto squire

did he see wild orbs of hair
imagine white skin
                          an abduction?

did he hear our rustling flesh
on my mother's custom
upholstered jungles and swamps

in the phillipines
she owned a moped   rode caribou

jumped out of trees
her machete ready to slice
the tee ting off of any man
who might want her sister

in the fire of questions
when the flash light hits our bodies
my father must prove our mixed skin
an i.d. a photo
a match

will he reach for the white throat

will he spin in the whirling jungle of
his wife's mats—

does he wish she were here?

Bridgette Wimberly

REVERSE DISCRIMINATION
ain't no such thing

Ain't no such thing as reverse discrimination
though some folks say its true
But ain't no reverse discrimination
'til all of us replace you

Not 'til the president and the vice president
congress and all the senate
are represented by the majority of us
with only a few of you in it

Not 'til the laws that govern this land
and the justices sworn to entrust
religiously gives us the upper-hand
and approaching the bench means facing us

Not 'til we fill every board room
the proverbial glass ceiling above your head
while banks and lending institutions
treat you like you're already dead

Don't wanna hear nothin' 'bout no reverse discrimination
to say it so don't make it true
'cause ain't no reverse discrimination
Not 'til you've walked a mile in our well worn shoes

Not 'til your great great grandma and grandpa
arrives on the shores of this nation
shackled to the bottom of a ship
slaves of our relations

Not 'til you're labeled three-fifths human
It's made illegal for you to read
Breed you, brand you, sell your children
the life that cattle out to pasture lead

Not 'til we use your free labor
work you from cradle to the grave
three-hundred years 'til an emancipation proclamation
makes you a so-called freed slave

Don't wanna hear nothin' 'bout no reverse discrimination
you can shout it 'til you're blue
But ain't no reverse discrimination
'til you've been through what we've been through

Not 'til living under Jim Crow laws
dictates you give black men your seat
While the best jobs listed under "for white only"
are to pick up trash and sweep the streets

Not 'til it takes an act from congress
the national guard in combat gear
just to escort your child to school
'cause we don't want no "whities" here

Not 'til you've marched hundreds of miles
to Birmingham, through Selma, and on to Washington DC
through rock throwing mobs, vicious dogs, and fire hoses
just trying to get some equality

Don't utter the word reverse discrimination
might as well fill your mouth with glue
'cause ain't no reverse discrimination
not 'til you've seen life from our view

Not 'til you know the fear of Emmit Till
Ku Klux Klan at your front door
lynch your husbands, sons, and brothers
for some black woman alleged to adore

Not 'til we bomb your homes and churches
kill your little girls as they pray
Castrate your men and rape your women
while the law looks clear the other way

Not 'til it takes the lives of freedom fighters
just to register you to vote
shot and buried in a river
where their bodies are left to bloat

Please don't insult us with reverse discrimination
for you must think we're all koo-koo
'cause ain't no reverse discrimination
Not with all this mess you put us through

Not 'til we practice red lining
force you to live in the slums
Give your children an inferior education
then label your off-spring genetically dumb

Not 'til the jails that fill this nation
overflow with your male youth
While drugs and guns infest your neighborhoods
strangling lives like a hangman's noose

Not 'til we brand you welfare deadbeats
and we hold the key to all the doors
Label all your men criminals
and all your women whores

Don't even think about reverse discrimination
for you bit off more than you can chew
'cause ain't no reverse discrimination
make the claim, then shame on you

Not 'til you're the last to be hired
and always the first to be let go
Work twice as hard, three times as long,
and never promoted, that's the status quo

Not 'til you must seek affirmative action
in hopes we'd hire just a few good men
MDs, PhDs, phi-beta-kappas
inferior quotas, just can't win

Not 'til you've gone through all that's mentioned
and you're still standing on your feet
Tired and bruised, disillusioned, weary
battle scars, but no defeat

Maybe then we can talk about reverse discrimination
But not an earlier second or two
'cause ain't no reverse discrimination
Not 'til you've lived this same hell too.

Yolanda Wisher

Ruby Flo

some folks like to plug her up

but she's the only woman i wait for
the only thing i can count on
my girl
Ruby Flo

queen of
solitude
repose
tranquillity
assurance
she do that shit alone
       & perfect
          complete
a deep red velvet carpet
plush with my insides
leadin her way

some folks like to plug her up
but you gotta let her be & love her

      what a comedian when she late
      what a trickster when she early
      what an actress when she heavy & dramatic
      what a child when she light & free

my girl
crimson layers
honeyed with fruitfulness
scented with prebirth musk
one after the other
unfoldin out of this delta called
Girl
    & then Woman
           then Mama

she be fertility
she be sacred
she be La Baker sweat
Shug Avery pee
granma's raspberry moon tea
independency

make me blessed
my woman
hooded & cloaked
in red
reminiscent of
the dawn after an eclipse
Chaka Khan's laden carmine lips
      singin—
"STAY"

some folks like to plug her up but
i like it when she come
like Red Ridin in the night
quick on her feet & just-a-stealin

other times she ease right out of me
real slow like a juke joint song
a Tony Brown tune
hummed even & low
so you know she there

but folks like to plug her up
won't let her speak
or take air from 'round their thighs

i said, some folks like to plug her up
but i sing her praises
      Ruby Flo…
          she do this shit alone & perfect

brazen &
sassy smellin
funky & fresh
my baby makin stew
only secret lips get to taste

she answer all my questions
hush all my doubts

i ask her—
"how come my man done left me"

& she say,
"cuz i ain't come 'round this month"

"& Ruby Flo
how come my man ain't sweet wit me this month?"

& she say,
"cuz i'ze fillin his space, chile"

"& Ruby Flo
how comes i git so low sometimes?"

& she say,
    "cuz i makes you still &
    you gots to be still to hear
    what you doing good
    & not so"

    "hear me, girl,"
    she say
    "i makes you interact
    wit all the stuff you don't need
    & then i helps you get rid of it

    no need for cryin or agitatin or fussin
    girl, don't fret these waters
    cuz they'll never drown you"

donchaknow
i be that magic called Creativity
i be daddy's twinkles
mixed wit granma's wrinkles
the potion that made you
the fluid named Passion in your pen

i'm the only ink been 'round since the Beginnin

    i be the Ruby Flo
    i be the Ruby Flo
    i be the Ruby Flowin

that jewel
anciently aggravatin undulatin
explodin like a sunburst
inside you
and fallin out of you like
weary petals droppin to the Earth

seekin
Rebirth

Vincent Woodard

bloodbrother ritual 2

last night last night
trembles like a
broken vase on my tongue—
how brief how brief we
bowed our heads and prayed/to
the silence that you crossed to
reach me where i trembled down the altar of your calf.
your lips' soft crust
peeling back at first
with mistrust
smelling for any sign that i would not
cup your head and
blow into the moon of your eyes.
asshole moistened lips
praying down the inside of your
bones
cuneiform words that would not erase
in the cool green pond of your beauty.
ash on my hand of your hand erasing me
and recreating candlelight upon your skin
blood brother i enter who
enters me twin
who does not cry out
who leads me out who leads me out
hand by hand/finger
by finger fucked
finger
whose eyes reflect my
dick lodged deep inside honey
whose breast is the breast of the
shore

fly free fly free
above me
hip inside the
healing sky of your hip
asshole moistened lips
parting even slower than my
heartbeats
inseparable
inseparable—

from you.

toni wynn

i value safety

my metropolitan ears
  want the freeway
  but it's too black here the freeway
is not black
  on saturday night
the white dedicated birds although like headlights
are also
  not black their loud talk uninterrupted
     by ten thousand radio waves

open shutters on morro bay
  bring saturday winter night air
    softer than my hands
  terrific pacific yards from here
 mimics the freeway so i can hear her
so i can then feel safe

Group E Collective Poem

We Are Thankful For Lucille Clifton

Because hers is
Because she is clean
Because she visited mud
Because she is wearing blue
Because she is the poet doctor
Because periods aren't endings
Because of the wisdom in her poetry
Because of the grace of *Good Woman*
Because she realizes the beauty in pain
Because she speaks to and from the soul
Because her care articulates my mother's
Because she lays marvelous, golden, eggs
Because of the *lesson of the falling leaves*
Because she wrote *leukemia as white rabbit*
Because I never would have started writing poetry

Because her wisdom is a blessing from the ancestors
Because she hold hands with other worlds seamlessly
Because she came into my life like a poem that shakes thunder
Because forgiveness, compassion and wisdom need a new icon
Because she makes a joke in her voice about the most serious thing
Because the voice of taboo is calm, normal, elegant and economical
Because sometimes the eyes have to see a holy aura to remember they exist
Because spirit knows which body to possess and which to give words to gargle
Because her poems reveal clean bones that have been ravished, but made whole
Because she has stood at the door of the house of used to be, but has not entered yet!
Because she knows how to organize thoughts into planets, planets into solar systems, into galaxies, that will become God.

Cave Canem

Cave Canem Renga

coffee broad shouldered
forgive rifts scars made from a belt
rain douses the morning   *Opal*

taste of snowdrops fill my mouth
steaming coffee warms insides   *Nancy*

swans floating on pond
cool breeze blowing across lake
squirrel crosses path   *Reginald*

water trickles onto stones
midnight sky of shooting stars   *Jacqueline*

ripe gardenia bloom
swinging loose by breeze and rain
sun looms into night   *Phyllis*

train drags daylight from the sky
spreads deep ochre in the land   *Toni*

woman knows the path
feet press fallen needles
a firefly   *Desiree*

twinkle twinkle june bug night
woman's Big Dipper hair net   *Cherryl*

unscarred snow falling,
disappearing onto tongues
the sweet taste of cold.   *Treasure*

we roll bundled on snow sheets
uncover patches of grass   Nelson

heads fall into ice
light cascades on melted drops
nappy edges shine   Mendi

leaves fall from giant oak trees
cast shadows on concrete curbs   Karen

the pool deck cement
warms under a girl's brown heels
wind knocks over glass   Eisa

grasping the long-handled net
a man skims bugs off water.   Jarvis

drowned mosquito shell
stiff in azure nylon mesh
fragile grounded kite   Douglas

the wind picking up flowers
stamen and pollen rain on down   Tracie

black couple on sheet
in the arts center's courtyard
breaking summer clouds   Lenard

Opal Palmer Adisa, Nancy Mebane Shakir, Reginald Lockett, Jacqueline Jones LaMon,
Phyllis McEwen, Toni Wynn, Desiree Cooper, Cherryl Floyd-Miller, Treasure Williams,
Nelson Demery III, Mendi Lewis Obadike, Karen Wade, Eisa Davis, Jarvis DeBerry,
Douglas Kearney, Tracie Morris, Lenard D. Moore (copyright 6/29/00)